SWINGS AND ROUNDABOUTS

The Professional Coaching Series

Series Editor: David Lane

Other titles in the series

The Art of Inspired Living: Coach Yourself with Positive Psychology
by Sarah Corrie

Business Coaching International: Transforming Individuals and Organizations
by Sunny Stout Rostron

Integrated Experiential Coaching: Becoming an Executive Coach
by Lloyd Chapman, with contributing author Sunny Stout Rostron

Coaching in the Family Owned Business: A Path to Growth
edited by Manfusa Shams and David A. Lane

Coaching in Education: Getting Better Results for Students, Educators, and Parents
edited by Christian van Nieuwerburgh

SWINGS AND ROUNDABOUTS

A Self-Coaching Workbook for Parents and Those Considering Becoming Parents

Anna Golawski, Agnes Bamford,
and Irvine Gersch

Routledge
Taylor & Francis Group
LONDON AND NEW YORK

First published 2013 by Karnac Books Ltd.

Published 2018 by Routledge
2 Park Square, Milton Park, Abingdon, Oxon OX14 4RN
711 Third Avenue, New York, NY 10017, USA

Routledge is an imprint of the Taylor & Francis Group, an informa business

British Library Cataloguing in Publication Data

A C.I.P. for this book is available from the British Library

ISBN-13: 9781780491233 (pbk)

Typeset by V Publishing Solutions Pvt Ltd., Chennai, India

We would like to dedicate this book to our children and grandchildren—Embla, Freya, and Markus; Klaudia and Oskar; Adam, Natalie, Joseph, Jonathan, Ben, Aaron, and Jacob; Emma, Ben, and, Bertie Max—for bringing joy, play, challenge, and love into our lives from the day they were born and for "raising us as parents and grandparents"

DISCLAIMER

This workbook is not intended to provide medical or psychological advice, or to take the place of medical advice and treatment from your GP or other medical specialist.

Readers are advised to consult their own doctors or other qualified professionals regarding the treatment of any conditions. The authors shall not be held liable or responsible for any misunderstanding or misuse of the information contained in this handbook, or for any loss, damage or injury caused or alleged to be caused directly or indirectly by any action discussed in this book. This handbook is not intended to diagnose, treat, cure or prevent any disorder but rather to facilitate readers making their own effective decisions and plans.

CONTENTS

LIST OF ACTIVITIES

ACKNOWLEDGEMENTS

First and foremost, we would like to thank our parents—Clive and Anne Dorthea Bamford and David and Stephanie Staples for being there for us always and for generously giving us love, praise, responsibility, and new experiences. It's not until we became parents ourselves that we truly appreciated how much you did for us as children—thank you!

Some of the activities in this book were inspired by those contained in the book "Seasons of Change" (Passmore & Pearson, 2011) which we wish to acknowledge with thanks for allowing their use and development.

We would like to thank colleagues in the School of Psychology at the University of East London for being the initiators behind this book and for directing and supporting us along the way. We would like to thank Alan Wilson MD of Develop Your Child for kindly allowing us to reprint some of the material from his book "The Parent Champion" and for his inspirational coaching attitude and passion for parents and children.

And finally we would like to express our sincere thanks to Barbara Gersch for kindly proof-reading the entire text and providing valuable advice.

COPYRIGHT PERMISSIONS

The authors of this book would like to acknowledge and thank the following people and organisations for their kind permission in allowing us to use the following quotes:

"Making the decision to have a child is momentous. It is to decide forever to have your heart walking outside your body"—From "A Boy I Once Knew: What a Teacher Learned From Her Student" by Elizabeth Stone. Reprinted by permission of Algonquin Books of Chapel Hill. All rights reserved.

"Coaching is about unlocking a person's potential to maximize their own performance"—From "Coaching For Performance" by Sir John Whitmore. Reprinted by permission of Nicolas Brealey Publishing.

"A hundred years from now it will not matter what my bank account was, the sort of house I lived in, or the kind of car I drove … but the world may be different because I was important in the life of a child."—From the poem "Within my Power—The Power of One Man" by Forest E Witcraft which appeared in the October 1950 issue of Scouting Magazine.

The quotation from David Barry is from *The Ice Cream Time Machine* (ebook published by Andrews UK), and is reproduced by kind permission.

The quotation from Stephen Covey is from *7 Habits of Highly Effective Families* (published by Simon & Schuster UK Ltd), and is reproduced by kind permission of the publisher.

ABOUT THE AUTHORS

Agnes Bamford, as a working mother of three children, can relate to the challenges and roller-coaster of emotions faced by most parents. Agnes has experienced the difference coaching can make for parents and families and she believes strongly in empowering parents to generate the relationship with their children that they dream of having. Agnes delivers parent-coaching courses in schools and corporations in addition to business coaching and group facilitation. She has written and contributed to coaching articles in the UK and Norway.

Agnes and Anna also wrote a chapter in the book "Coaching and Mentoring in Education: Getting Better Results for Students, Educators and Parents", published by Karnac Books in June 2012.

Irvine Gersch BA(Hons) PGCE DipEd Psych PhD FBPsS FHEA FRSA CPsychol HCPC registered. Irvine is a professor of educational and child psychology at the University of East London. Following his first degree in psychology, he went on to qualify as a teacher and educational psychologist, and complete a PhD on child behaviour and school leadership. He has held positions as a teacher, principal educational psychologist, university lecturer, and programme director for the training of educational psychologists. He is a chartered psychologist and holds fellowships of the BPS, HEA, and RSA. He has published widely in the field of listening to children, run many parent training sessions, and continues to enjoy learning enormously from, and being with, his own children and grandchildren.

Anna Golawski is a dedicated mum to two young children and successfully manages to run her own coaching business. After spending many years in the corporate world she totally understands the tears and triumphs that go hand-in-hand with being a working parent.

Anna is described by her clients as being highly effective and having a natural, down-to-earth approach that helps them get the most out of their coaching sessions and fulfil their goals and ambitions, and increase their confidence in parenting abilities. Anna works with individuals, companies and the education sector and is also a mentor for The Prince's Trust. She has written several coaching articles for magazines and business publications.

SERIES EDITOR'S FOREWORD

The swings and roundabouts of parenting—from reflection to action

We are delighted to bring you *Swings and Roundabouts: A Self-Coaching Workbook for Parents and Those Considering Becoming Parents* by our colleagues Anna Golawski, Agnes Bamford, and Irvine Gersch.

As part of the Professional Coaching Series we have always had in mind the varied contexts in which coaching adds value. This has included the workplace, family business, and education. There are more contexts we plan to cover in future editions.

One theme that has informed us in making choices for inclusion in the series is the power of guided self-coaching. Our very first book in the series, *The Art of Inspired Living* by Sarah Corrie focused on the use of positive psychology as a self-coaching tool. We return to the power of self-coaching in this book. It is very much a practical book to help parents and parents-to-be to consider the choices available to them.

It is based on good practice in coaching and takes as a starting point reflection as a way to frame choice processes. By learning to reflect with others on our choices as parents we can begin to open up options. What otherwise would seem daunting becomes less so. However, the authors do not encourage reflection as an end in itself but to help you as a parent reading this book to move from reflection to action. The questions they pose assist that process. They are able to draw upon the literature from coaching, childcare, and their own experience as professionals and parents. They speak with authority but without ego. They do not pretend to know all the answers or promote one view. True to the fundamentals of coaching, they help you to find the answers that make sense for you. They do not seek to create parents in their mould but help you to formulate your own approach.

The exercises in the book are there to generate your reflections on the questions posed and to create new questions of your own for further reflection. From this starting point they take you through a range of activities and approaches you can use as a parent. They point to other sources, which you will find valuable, and sources of support for when you cannot manage by yourself—or just need others to share your concerns.

As you work through the book (at the appropriate time), you will be encouraged to create a personal plan. This will help to manage the frustrations of parenting as well as provide a context for its joys.

While it is considered a truism that parenting is the most important job we do for those who are lucky enough to have the privilege of being a parent—its importance is clear. For those who make other decisions (or have the decision made for them), they are still part of the environment in which children grow and thrive. There is an African saying—a community raises a child—and the authors encourage parents to seek the support of others. We are all responsible for our children and as a community need to support those who have the privilege of being parents.

For many years I worked with children and their parents to help them to deal with times of distress and challenge. I found I learned much from them and was constantly amazed by the power that self-reflection unleashed. The authors embody that power in the gentle and effective way that they lead us through the swings and roundabouts of parenting.

As a professional I commend the book as an important contribution to our understanding of the value of coaching to the task of parenting. As a parent I wish I had this book available to me in the past. However, as a grandparent I have found much to help me to reflect on how I might gently help my own children in their role as parents.

For many reasons I am delighted to introduce the work of Anna Golawski, Agnes Bamford, and Irvine Gersch to you in the Professional Coaching Series. I wholeheartedly recommend it to you.

Professor David A Lane
Professional Development Foundation

FOREWORD

Sir John Whitmore PhD

Anna, Agnes, and Irvine have written this excellent and much needed book for parents and potential parents. In fact the book covers a very broad spectrum of issues that may emerge for all people entering, or well into, the child-bearing age. It ranges from the choice to have a baby, pregnancy, and birth, to caring for and, dare I say it, coping with a child up to 4 years old.

There are plenty of books available that give advice to such people but I suggest this is much more valuable than all of them because it is rooted in the principle of self-coaching. Our whole culture is evolving now from doing what we are told by an authority towards taking self-responsibility for our choices, actions, consequences, and circumstances. It works far better this way, and we ourselves build our pleasure, joy, success and self-belief by so doing.

No two people in the world are the same physically or psychologically and they are far happier and more effective when they do things their own natural way. Since we may be less accustomed to that because we were told too much by others, this book is a self-coaching manual filled with countless coaching questions for readers to ask themselves. They are thereby provoked into thinking more deeply about immediate questions, but also into long term deep thinking about parenting. This enables them to make the choices that they think will work best for them, now and later. As your reading and time passes, the questions are sequentially appropriate.

Nobody but experienced coaches with their own child-bearing experience would be able to come up with such a complete selection of questions from the simple to the most profound. They have done so brilliantly, and that, and they, will benefit many parents and children in future.

It is possible that some readers at first might feel daunted by the number and the depth of the questions, the time and work involved, and the challenges that they may raise—but they need not be. A reader can freely choose what questions to ignore, and those they ask themselves, and when, and in what sequence they do so. Parent readers are given space to write their answers but they are not obliged to do so; just thinking about them now and later may be sufficient for some and incomplete for others.

Triggered by the significance and depth of these questions, some readers might want to take self-coaching a step further by thinking up and asking themselves those questions that are most relevant and important to them personally. Simply identifying those questions we most want to ask ourselves, or even those that we might not want to be asked by another, can be very valuable. You might soon find yourself coaching a parenting friend. It is a pleasant, easy, helpful, natural process to use to assist others.

I could easily write more here because of my enthusiasm for this book, but it is their book and they have done it so much better than I could. Read on.

INTRODUCTION

> "A hundred years from now it will not matter what my bank account was, the sort of house I lived in, or the kind of car I drove...but the world may be different because I was important in the life of a child".
>
> —*Forest E. Witcraft*

This coaching workbook is the result of a collaboration between the University of East London and two parent-coaches. Agnes and Anna are parents who have been on a journey of "swings and roundabouts" ourselves, experiencing the highs and lows of having children. Having encountered difficulties in knowing the best way to parent and raise our children at various stages of development, a state of affairs which was not made easier by the conflicting advice in the media, made us unsure of our own parenting skills and undermined confidence in our abilities. This was one of the reasons we entered into the field of parent-coaching. We were trained coaches who wanted to use our coaching skills and experience as parents to help ourselves and other parents get the understanding and trust in themselves to be the parents they dream of being. Parents often feel alone and we found that running courses for them created a space where they could share experiences with each other as well as experiment with different ways of parenting. Parent-coaching has made us become much more aware of how we are as parents and how we can affect our children. It is our intention to give back to you some of the awareness we gained ourselves in this self-coaching book.

Its aim is for you to feel empowered and competent as a parent or potential parent. We are not trying to offer you yet another advice book on parenting to drown out your own instincts; rather we are here to encourage you to trust your instinct on what is best for you, your child, and your situation and to have the confidence to take that action.

We start off with a chapter on self-reflection and life goals with the idea that you can coach yourself on whether you wish to become a parent or not and how this fits in with your life goals. (If you are already pregnant or have children you may find this section useful for self-reflection in general).

We wish to make you feel more empowered whether you are considering having a child or are already a parent and to understand that you have choices. There may be more than two answers to a problem and we aim to help you to believe in yourself making the choice as we recognise that there is a balance to be found between career aspirations and starting a family. Knowing that there is never going to be another situation out there that is just like yours may enable you to believe in yourself.

Although feeling your way in the dark may be frowned upon, we believe that parents need space and time to do just that. We also believe that every child is a unique, special individual from whom we need to learn as well as teach.

> "Despite the range of parenting advice and methods available, quite often natural parental instinct is usually the best thing for children".
>
> —*Agnes Bamford & Anna Golawski*

Having a child marks a fundamental change in our lifestyle and sense of self. It may be that you have six months of utter chaos and then you begin to find your way through it, which is quite normal (see our baby adjustment graph in Chapter Four). Ultimately what you learn is that whatever approach works best for you and your child is the best approach and this may be completely different from what works for someone else. Focusing on what is really important—love, consistency, making time for your children, listening to them, as well as learning from them—is what really matters. As many parents will already have experienced, parenting has its ups and downs, and is not all plain sailing or as romantic as we see in the magazines—thus we have decided to recognise this important point in our title—SWINGS AND ROUNDABOUTS.

How to use the workbook and the coaching approach

The workbook is based on the principle that we can all learn how to be really great parents for our own children.

> "Everything depends on upbringing".
>
> —*Leo Tolstoy*

The workbook is intended to be used as a practical tool to help you extend your understanding of the choices available to you as a parent. It provides a range of activities and approaches you can apply to yourself as a parent. These can be completed on your own or with your partner (please don't be constrained by our use of the term partner; you may just as well have these conversations with a close family member or friend) based on your personal preference.

The activities within the workbook invite you to write your reflections. The exercises are intended to allow you time to formulate your own personal plan through self-reflection. Each one, where appropriate, is accompanied by coaching questions and provides guidance for those of you who are either considering having children, who are pregnant or who have young children. It can also be used by those of you who have specific requirements or interests in one of the topics areas.

We have taken a step-by-step approach to change and self-improvement. Each section has general information as well as activities. Each activity has questions to aid self-reflection and a notes section, allowing you to record thoughts, future activities, and future goals.

Depending upon your requirements you may prefer to work through the workbook systematically and do the activities in the order they are presented or you may prefer to pick topics of particular interest to you while ignoring others.

What do we mean by coaching?

There are many ways to define the term 'coaching'. Some emphasise its learning nature, while others suggest that it is more about facilitation.

Within this workbook we hold the view that:

> "Coaching is about unlocking a person's potential to maximize their own performance".
>
> —*Sir John Whitmore, 2009*

The self-coaching activities offer thought-provoking questions and opportunities for conversations with your partner. We look at 'What does the parent want to achieve?' and 'What are the measures of success?' The aim is to help you to make the right choices for you and your family. The activities have been designed to draw out information from the reader. The approach is evidence-based and builds upon our research at the University of East London.

We have adapted this approach to form a guide to self-coaching, drawing upon coaching techniques. We have used open questions to develop self-awareness, responsibility and to encourage your thought processes.

The workbook is designed to facilitate, stimulate, and support learning through self-reflection.

We have outlined the GROW model (Whitmore, 2003) below as an approach to self-discovery. A useful metaphor for the GROW model is planning a journey. First, we need the postcode of our destination (Our Goal) and the home postcode or where we are now (Reality). We can then Google the possible routes we could take. The results provided offer the choice of routes,for example the quickest route, the motorway route or the route which avoids road works (Options).We now have all of the information if we decide to make the journey (Way Forward).

Destination	–	Goal
Home	–	Reality
Possible routes	–	Options
Making the journey	–	Way forward

The grow model applied to parenting:

What do I want for me and my family?
What is happening now?
What else could I do?
What are the ups and downs of the different choices I have available?
What will I do, and when?

The GROW (Goal, Reality, Options, and Way Forward) model is the format used within the coaching activities to increase personal awareness of the choices we face and to help you think about what you want. We take the view we are not expert parents—far from it. Indeed, we start with the proposition that you, as the parent, are the best expert in respect to your own child. Instead, we hope to offer some useful questions which will help you become better informed parents who are making informed choices which fit your wider values and beliefs and your family needs. This approach does not offer advice or direction. It provides a framework for you to discover your own way forward as a parent.

Workbook objectives

The objectives of this parent-workbook are:

- To provide exercises that help you clarify what you want
- To identify options and choices you have as a parent
- To help you better understand yourself as a parent
- To offer topics to explore and discuss with your partner
- To offer a wealth of resources that you will find useful—links to books, websites, charities, and organisations
- To help you raise happy, secure, confident children.

The parent workbook structure

There are five main chapters:

1. Self-reflection and choosing whether to have a baby or not
2. Pregnancy
3. Birth
4. First year
5. Next steps (years 1–4)

Areas explored

Theme	*Topics*	*Page*
4. First year	8. Separation	78
	9. Children's needs	79
	10. Milestones	82
	11. Weaning	83
	12. The development of language and thinking	84
	13. Maintaining your relationship with your partner	86
	14. Letting your feelings be known	87
	15. Finding special time for yourself	88
	16. Finding time for romance	90
	17. New mothers: getting your body back	91
	18. Work/Life balance	92
	19. Managing finances when returning to work	96
	20. Choosing childcare	97
	21. Reflections on being a parent	99
	22. Chapter summary	102
5. Next steps	1. How will you manage household tasks?	103
	2. What sort of parent do you want to be?	106
	3. The importance of play	118
	4. Praise and sanctions	119
	5. Communicating with our children; listening	122
	6. Dealing with our own and our children's feelings	123
	7. Approaches to discipline and children's behaviour	125
	8. Choices and consequences	128
	9. Giving children responsibility	128
	10. The labels our children wear	130
	11. Ready to do it all again?	132
	12. Chapter summary	133

CHAPTER ONE

Choosing to have a baby or not

In this section we will explore if you want to become a parent, what you want to get from it, and what you want to contribute.

The first step in becoming able to deal with these challenges is to deepen our understanding of ourselves and how we are likely to respond. In doing so, we can also become more accepting of change and increasingly able to build personal resilience. You will also benefit from going through the self-reflection exercises in this chapter when you are pregnant or if you are already a parent. It's worth recognising that the more you know yourself and look after yourself, the more you are able to look after your children, and the happier you are likely to be. By taking time to acknowledge yourself you will be giving your children a valuable message about your worth.

We will be taking you on a journey of reflection about what's important to you in your life, as well as dealing with change and looking at whether or not to get pregnant, pros and cons of having a baby, parenting styles and practical considerations you may want to take into account when making such a big life-changing choice.

Based on feedback and our own experience as coaches and psychologists, we have found it helps if people write down their answers, rather than just think about them. The workbook has been designed to follow a self-coaching approach. We suggest that you talk about the questions with your partner or another close friend/family member, then make notes to summarise your thinking.

Please select the exercises or questions which are relevant to your own situation. Some of them are designed to get you to think about particular issues in a number of different ways. There are no right or wrong answers; rather this book is designed to help you explore your own personal situation and increase your self-awareness.

Self-awareness

> "He who knows others is wise. He who knows himself is enlightened".
>
> —*Lao Tzu*

Self-awareness is useful to us throughout our lives, and the ability to self-reflect is particularly useful during personal change and transition, including the change that having a baby would mean to you. Self-awareness includes a recognition of our personality, our strengths and weaknesses, our likes and dislikes.

Self-awareness can help individuals to recognise personal stresses and pressures. It is also often a prerequisite for effective communication and interpersonal relations, as well as for developing empathy.

In simple terms, self-awareness is about trying to understand who we really are, why we do the things we do and how we do them. By becoming more self-aware we can gain a greater degree of control over how we are operating in the present, instead of reacting to events without consideration of the consequences of our decisions.

Listed below are some of the benefits of increasing your self-awareness:

- Gaining more control around pregnancy and birth
- Being more flexible and confident in our approach to raising children
- Helping ourselves to deal with challenges in a more positive and less anxious way
- Interacting better, communicating more effectively, and understanding our relationships with others—including our partners and children—more fully
- Making better decisions around parenting
- Reducing our stress levels
- Getting more out of life.

Activity 1.1: Where am I now?

The activity below is designed to start the thought process about who you are and where you are in your life.

Answer the following questions:

Where am I now (in my life) with regards to work, social life, relationships?

Where do I want to be?
If I decide to become a parent, how do I want to be?

What do I want to get out of this workbook (we suggest that you try to be as specific as possible)?

What is important to me?

Very rarely do we take time for self-reflection. A good starting point for coaching yourself, whether you are considering having children or if you are already a parent and want to understand yourself better, is to explore what is really important to you.

In order to make good decisions both as a parent, and in life as a whole, we all need to have a clear understanding of what is important to us—alongside understanding our values, beliefs and also our attitudes towards major issues.

From our experience of coaching hundreds of people from a wide variety of backgrounds, we have found no two people are exactly identical. Each has their own experience and point of view.

For some, relationships have a central importance in their life, while others value time spent on their own.

In the two columns in the table on the following page, list the areas that are most important to you in life as a whole and what you think will be important to you as a parent.

Activity 1.2: Areas of my life that are important to me

My life as a whole at present	*Me as a parent in the future*

Reflecting on your answers above, what insights have you discovered?

Please write them down here if you would like to:

Activity 1.3: Knowing yourself

Here are ten questions which will help you to think about who you really are. Of course we could have come up with a hundred, but hopefully this is a useful place to start.

What are your strengths?
What are your weaknesses?
How do your friends describe you?
What types of activities did you enjoy doing when you were a child?
What do you enjoy doing most now?

What is the most important thing to you in your life? Do you feel you have a particular purpose? What is this?
What are your dreams and goals for the future?
In what situations do you feel most stressed?
In what situations do you feel most relaxed?
What qualities do you like to see in people?

Change

> "It is not the strongest of the species that survive, nor the most intelligent, but the ones most responsive to change".
>
> —*Charles Darwin*

Change is all around us. It is constant. Our current situation is merely a snapshot within that process of change and regeneration. Our attitude to change is central to our ability to thrive. The ability to handle change is an important life skill. There are a number of ways in which we can help you to understand and work with change.

Sometimes we can decide whether we want to make a change or not. However, there are situations where change is imposed, the birth of a child being one of them.

Even though we are all aware that we will have to make changes when we have children, the birth of a child changes our lives completely, and that can be a shock. Research suggests that the primary reason for this reaction is that change, when imposed upon an individual, is more difficult to deal with as it takes away one's sense of control. This has been shown to have a significant influence on physical and psychological well-being. If you find that you or your partner is pregnant "without having made the choice", you may find the initial phases of pregnancy and birth more difficult.

The pregnancy news emotional change curve

The original work on the change curve came from research attributed to Dr Elizabeth Kubler-Ross. It has been used to highlight the emotions for various changing events or transitions in life and can be used in some way to describe the fluctuating feelings of having a child, particularly if it is unplanned.

We have developed our own model of the change curve to illustrate the emotions encountered when you find out you are pregnant.

Diagram 1: The pregnancy news emotional change curve

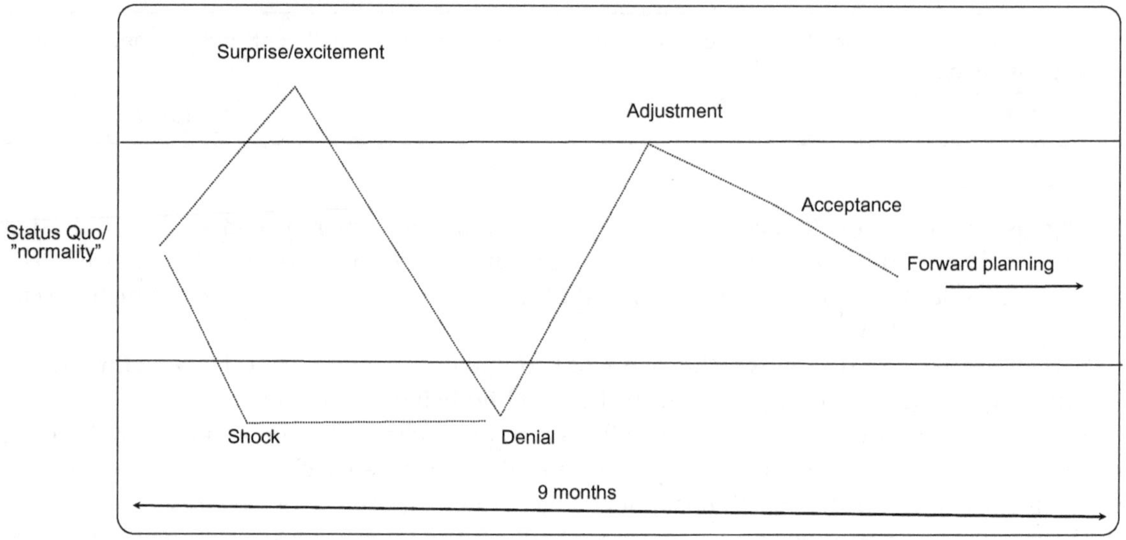

The curve and its stages should not be seen as a rigid series of sequential or uniformly timed steps throughout your or your partner's pregnancy and early months of being a parent. Rather, it is purely a guide. Some people do not experience all the stages and whether you do or not will largely depend on whether your baby is planned. Each individual will experience the curve in their own way. It should be noted that these feelings are normal and sometimes can seem quite conflicting.

When you realise it is normal to have these conflicting feelings and emotions you may feel better about yourself and better equipped to deal with your situation. The following sections of this book will help you with this.

Pregnancy news—emotional curve.	
Stage	*Interpretation*
Status quo/normality	The status quo, life carries on as usual, there are no imminent signs of change.
Surprise/excitement	This stage is categorised by feelings of surprise and excitement. You may feel overwhelmed with the news of the pregnancy, you may feel excited, or relieved if this is a long-awaited pregnancy.
Shock	Some people may feel shocked at finding out that they or their partner are pregnant—and probably more so if the pregnancy wasn't planned. Awareness that this is part of the natural process can help individuals to deal with the emotions and make plans for the future.
Denial	There is a conscious or unconscious refusal to accept the fact that you or your partner are pregnant. It can be seen as a defence mechanism. This is perfectly natural. The danger is that some individuals can become locked in this stage. In a pregnancy context, this could manifest itself as disbelief that you are actually going to be parents.
Adjustment/Realisation	This stage will vary according to the person's situation and for a lot of people shows that the person/couple has begun to accept the reality of expecting a baby and the lifestyle changes that will need to be made.
Acceptance	This phase can be seen as the start of the new mindset. The individual starts to examine scenarios and tests what these options could offer if accepted.
Forward planning	Again, this stage varies according to the person's situation, although broadly it is an indication that there is some clarity around the circumstances and objectivity. At this stage, you are likely to make decisions about your lifestyle and how having a baby is going to change your current situation and start to put in place some plans and actions.

Activity 1.4: Managing the stress and anxiety of change

Change can feel overwhelming, especially at first. Answering the questions over the following pages will help you to clarify your response to change. It is often helpful to think things through carefully in a structured way.

Do I know enough about what it means to have a baby? If not, what do I need to know?
How can I find out more information?
Who can I ask?

Do I understand how the change will work?
How will it impact on me?
How will it impact on my work and my relationship with my partner?
Are there areas which remain unclear? If so, where and how can I obtain clarification?

The biggest benefit of the change curve is that it helps us to understand that our reaction to change is natural. Many people will have a similar set of emotional responses when dealing with the change of lifestyle that having a baby will bring.

Activity 1.5: Life goals

In planning our future we need to recognise where we are starting from.

You may have already thought about the journey into your future; from where you are now to where you want to be. If not, here are some questions to get you started.

Try to be as detailed as you can in responding to the questions.

Remember: it's fine if your answers are the same for two or even three of the questions. Try to be specific.

What would you like to be, or be doing, in:
5 years?
10 years?

15 years?

20 years?

What are the three most important things you would like to achieve over the next ten years?
1
2
3

What do you need to do to make these things happen?
1
2
3

How would children affect your life goals?
How would children affect your relationship?
How would children affect your way of life/life style/career?

Should I (we) get pregnant?

> "A baby will make love stronger, days shorter, nights longer, bankroll smaller, home happier, clothes shabbier, the past forgotten and the future worth living for".
>
> —*author unknown*

We think it is useful to weigh up the pros and cons of having a baby as objectively as we can before taking the first step towards conception. First, we need to decide whether there are benefits in staying as we are. It is useful to acknowledge what these benefits are, and to examine whether those we expect to get as a result of having a baby will be greater.

While it may be useful to deliberately consider the pros and cons of having a baby, we do acknowledge that ultimately emotions and a ticking body clock may override any seemingly rational decisions.

We also want to stress that we are not dictating the rights or wrongs of having a baby, rather we are asking questions to facilitate the decision making process, especially when lifestyle and career aspirations need to be considered.

We have provided four key questions in Activity 1.7 which may help you explore the potential advantages and disadvantages of your choices. These will also help you to minimise any negative surprises. With each question, be strict with yourself. As soon as you've written an answer, ask yourself: '… and what else?' Keep asking until you cannot generate any more reasons.

> "Making the decision to have a child is momentous. It is to decide forever to have your heart go walking outside your body".
>
> —*Elisabeth Stone*

Activity 1.6: Should I (we) get pregnant?

What would happen if I (we) did decide to have a baby?
What would happen if I (we) didn't?
What are the longer term benefits if I (we) have a child?
What are the longer term disadvantages of having a child?

These questions allow a surprising number of additional insights to surface.

If you are part of a couple you may want to consider at this stage what your expectations are in relation to having a baby. The more you manage to communicate your expectations, the better well-equipped are you to face the changes involved for you in becoming parents.

Diversity: the changing face of families

We live in a diverse society where there are many varied types of families, including same-sex couples, single parents, blended families (one or both of you has children from a previous relationship) and parents who are from different cultures to each other and to the main culture they live in. In addition to the above considerations for wanting a baby, same-sex couples, or those with a different cultural background and single potential parents will have additional decisions to consider.

> "Whether you are a single parent family, two parent family, step or blended family, yours is as real and valid as any other".
>
> —*Agnes Bamford & Anna Golawski*

If you are in a lesbian relationship you may need to discuss who the birth mother will be and who the sperm donor will be. Regarding the latter point, is this person to be anonymous or will the father be involved in the upbringing of the child?

If you are a single woman who wants a child but is not in a relationship you may also need to consider sperm donation in order to conceive and whether this is done anonymously. We suggest that you consider the section on what having a baby means to you and think about the support network around you in bringing up a child.

If you are in a blended family, you may need to consider the possible impact on the existing children of having new siblings. How will you manage the new family dynamics for example? What do you need to do to communicate with the children and reassure them if they have concerns? How will you handle any jealousy? How will you and your new partner integrate your families together?

If you are from a different culture you may speak another language; you may want to reflect on whether you wish to bring up your child to be bi-lingual. There is substantial evidence that speaking more than one language is beneficial for a child. You may wish to consider these three questions with your partner: What effort is required to make your child speak your mother tongue? What are the benefits? How does your partner (if he/she does not speak your language) feel about this?

Pros and cons of having a baby/another baby

The decision to have a baby is an intensely personal one, and there is no right or wrong answer. Sometimes events overtake us.

There are many factors to consider when planning a family, such as:

- Are you both willing to become parents?
- Are you ready to have a child—financially, emotionally, physically?
- Will the baby be naturally conceived, would you wish to use IVF or adopt?

Many parents-to-be romanticise about having a baby and don't realise the major impact that having a baby can entail. Everything from your career, social life, lifestyle, relationship with your partner and extended family will be affected (in good and challenging ways).

Some people have firm ideas as to whether they want to become a parent or not, and sometimes how many children they ideally would like to have. Others may feel less certain and making a list of pros and cons of having a baby may help clarify the situation for them.

Activity 1.7: Pros and cons of having a baby/another baby

Make a list of the pros and cons of having a baby and how it may affect your current lifestyle.

When one of us did this we consulted friends, colleagues, and wider family to listen to their experiences and build up a wider range of perspectives. You may wish to do the same (again, remember that emotions may override rational decisions).

Pros	*Cons*

Once you have drawn up the list, take time to reflect on it and identify what surprises there were and if you feel differently about whether you want a baby, bearing in mind that your gut instinct may override any rational thoughts!

Please write down your reflections:

When do you want your child to be born?

Many parents don't have a choice as to when they try to conceive—some people get pregnant immediately whereas for others it can take months if not years. Many couples find that they are expecting a baby without having planned it.

However, there are some factors that are worth taking into consideration if you have the choice of when to try to conceive:

You may want to avoid Christmas or other times which are busy and expensive times of the year, or avoid having babies in July or August as it means they will be one of the youngest in their year at school. It is not surprising that research evidence shows that it takes a while for the younger child in a year to catch up with the performance of older children born in September or October.

If you have a definite time of year when you would like to have a baby you may want to think about when you try to conceive.

There are other health issues to consider when having a baby—ages of the parents, for example, and the fact that after the age of 36 there are increased health risks for mothers. However, it should be noted that more and more women are having babies in their later thirties, and forties. We would recommend speaking to your doctor or midwife if you have any concerns.

That said, it is rarely possible to time births with great precision and there is no "perfect" time to have a baby.

IVF or adoption?

For some people, getting pregnant does not happen as easily as they may have hoped. You may like to consider what you would do, or how you might feel, if you don't get pregnant.

Activity 1.8: Alternatives to getting pregnant

What if we don't get pregnant?
When should we seek advice from a doctor?

After six to twelve months of trying, some couples decide to consult their doctor.

Your doctor may offer tests as well as discussing with you other options. For some couples this may ultimately lead them to consider other options such as IVF or adoption.

IVF treatment can be costly and can affect some people emotionally. If this happens, we would suggest that you and your partner talk openly about your feelings about the choices you have.

Unplanned pregnancy

Just as some people may struggle to conceive, others may find themselves unexpectedly pregnant and have to decide whether they are able and willing to keep their baby.

We suggest that you seek specialist support in such a situation to discuss your options in order to make the right decision for you and your circumstances. At the end of the book is a list of useful resources.

If you are willing to keep the baby, this is your ultimately your decision, however it is worth discussing the situation with friends, family or partner as soon as possible.

Consider how having the baby can be a great experience.

How did your parents bring you up?

In the same way that there is no perfect time to have a baby, there are no such things as perfect parents. This may be a time for you to reflect on how you were parented yourself.

Psychological research into child-rearing has resulted in identifying three main stereotypes of parenting (Berk, 2008).

Assertive parenting

This style involves setting rules and boundaries for children whilst also showing them love and affection. Parents listen patiently to their child's viewpoints and include them in family decisions. The parents are in control, but allow their children the freedom to develop and make mistakes. Children are lively and happy, and have high self-esteem and self-control.

Authoritarian parenting

This style of parenting sets high demands on children and places a high value on conforming to rules and discipline. Parents tend to have an attitude of "do as I say". Children are found to be anxious and withdrawn and can react with hostility when frustrated.

Permissive parenting

This style involves being nurturing and accepting of children's misbehaviour, but it avoids making demands and therefore lacks control. The children are allowed to make their own decisions before they are capable of doing so. There is a lack of discipline, boundaries and structure. Children tend to be immature, disobedient and rebellious and have low self-esteem (Berk, 2008).

Nobody can be expected to be "perfect" parents. Every parent fluctuates along the continuum from authoritarian to permissive. Indeed, many parents rightly adopt a flexible response according to the situation, bearing in mind the context. This might be called 'situational parenting', utilising the most effective style for any given situation and issue, ensuring that the response is fit for purpose. In the following exercise we suggest you consider where you are on the 'average' day. Of course this is not a scientific exercise—our aim is to help you think about your parenting style and how it fits with your aims and with those of your partner.

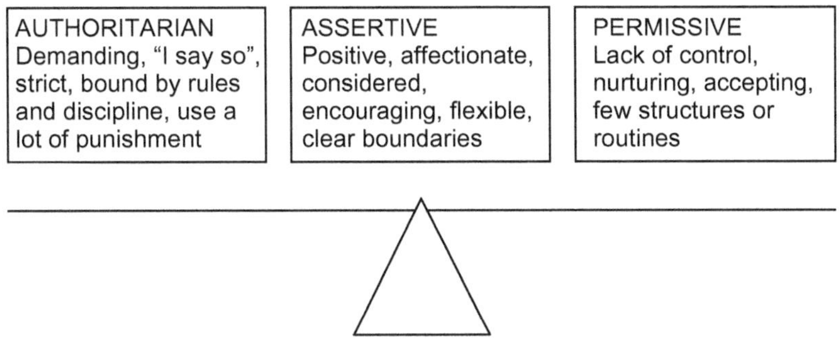

Activity 1.9: Parenting styles

Use the scale diagram above to think about how you were parented.

What effect has this had on you?
How might your childhood experiences influence how you view raising children?
How does this fit with your partner's style?

What changes may you want to make if any?

It is also important to take into account that the parent-child relationship is a two-way street, especially over time. Perhaps children's own characteristics contribute to the ease with which the parents can adopt an assertive style.

Nutrition and fitness for pregnancy

Once a woman has found out she is pregnant there is a great incentive to eat well for both her health and fitness, and for the wellbeing and development of her unborn baby.

It is also worth paying attention to nutrition and fitness in the months leading up to conception, these being factors which can play a part in the woman's ability to conceive.

Indeed, we now know about the enormous impact of parental, and even grandparental, nutrition and health upon the baby's future wellbeing and development. The following factors are particularly critical:

- Parental nutrition
- Air breathed—avoidance of active or passive smoking
- Stress, particularly in the mother.

A summary of the detailed research evidence is contained in an excellent BBC Radio 4 series entitled The First 1000 Days by Dr M Porter (2011) and is available on podcasts; it is recommended. In short, the first 1000 days of the baby's life, from conception, in the womb, and beyond, have a critical effect on the child's future health, welfare and longevity.

In completing the food diary described below, consideration should be given to smoking, alcohol, and stress levels.

These aspects of life may need specific review and attention.

You might like to use a food diary as a tool to help you reflect on how healthy your current diet and lifestyle is.

Activity 1.10: Food diary for pregnancy

	Monday	*Tuesday*	*Wednesday*	*Thursday*	*Friday*	*Saturday*	*Sunday*
Breakfast							
Lunch							
Dinner							
Snacks							
Drinks							
Alcohol							

At the end of the week review your diet with your partner or a family member and consider whether you wish to make any changes.

1. Do I need to review my diet and nutritional intake?
2. Do I need to review any habits relating to smoking (through direct or passive smoking, such as being in a smoky environment)?
3. Do I need to review alcohol use?
4. Are my ways of stress managment effective or is a review needed? If so, who is best to discuss this with me?

Supplements

The general advice is that taking a supplement of folic acid one to three months before conception and for the first trimester will reduce the risk of spina bifida. Other suggested supplements are vitamin B12 and iron which are used to make red blood cells for the baby and mother.

Before taking any supplements, you should seek advice from your doctor.

Activity 1.11: Supplements

Do you feel you would benefit from taking supplements? If so, how?
What supplements, if any, are you considering taking?

Fitness and exercise

In addition to a healthy diet, it is recommended that women who are planning on getting pregnant also do exercise to ensure they are physically fit and healthy.

Activity 1.12: Exercise in pregnancy

For a week, track how much exercise you do in your daily routine and note it in the box below. After a week, review this and see if there are any changes that you would like to make and note them in your plan.

Day	*Current exercise*	*Planned changes (if any)*
Monday		
Tuesday		
Wednesday		
Thursday		
Friday		
Saturday		
Sunday		

What changes, if any, would you like to make in the exercise you take?
How will you fit this into your current lifestyle?

Activity 1.13: Fitness goals

If you do wish to take part in a fitness/exercise programme, the following questions may help you achieve your goal:

What are your fitness goals? (e.g., a certain weight, fitness level or dress size) By what date?
What is your current level of fitness? Are there any medical/health issues that you need to consider?

What can you do to achieve your goal? How often would you do the activities needed to achieve your goal?
What is the first step you are going to take in achieving your goal?

How will having a child affect your family budget?

> "Mother Nature, in her infinite wisdom has installed within each of us a powerful biological instinct to reproduce; this is her way of assuring that the human race, come what may, will never have any disposable income".
>
> —*David Barry*

Having a baby is going to add to your day-to-day living costs, from food and clothing to childcare fees. Some parents also review their long term savings plans for costs such as weddings or university fees.

Try to think of your financial planning as if you were running a business. You may already have a firm hold and understanding of your finances and may not feel that this section is relevant. If you already plan your finances much of this will be familiar.

If you do not, we would suggest that you look at your current outgoings (expenditure) in comparison with your current income. You will be able to produce a budget planner. This will allow you to get a better understanding of what your day-to-day life is costing and identify future changes in costs and how this may impact your current lifestyle. It will also help in returning to work and calculating childcare costs vs. salary.

We are not suggesting that you plan your annual expenditure to within £5, but maybe trying to be within £200 would be helpful. By using a budget planner, like the one below, you can get a better understanding of what life costs. This can help you decide whether the balance between your income and expenditure is right for you, whether you and your partner need to go back to work full-time or part-time after your baby is born, and how this may affect your work–life balance and other family commitments. Remember, it is always easy to under-estimate costs and over-estimate prospective income, forgetting about deductions.

Activity 1.14: My financial planner

On the following pages we have set up a six month financial planner for you to complete.

For the purposes of this activity, the terms running down the left hand column are defined as follows:

Income	
Net Salaries	Family salaries, benefits, child tax credits
Others	Any tax refunds, bonuses, assets, rental income
Outgoings	
Transport	Car purchase, fuel, service/MOT, road tax, repairs, insurance, public transport costs
Household	Water rates, council tax, gas, electricity, telephone, TV licence
Food	Food and drink
Insurance	Contents, buildings, life policies, medical
Home and garden	Maintenance/DIY, heating, furniture, garden furniture/equipment/maintenance
Holidays	Hotels, travel fares, insurance
Social	Dining out, entertainment
Dependents	Allowances, gifts, maintenance payments, school fees
Personal	Clothes, hobbies, gifts, charity, medical, dental, optician, subscriptions, fares
Miscellaneous	Bank charges, contingencies, long term savings plans, pension
New baby	Equipment, clothes, toys, cot, pram, car seat
Childcare	Nursery, childminder, holiday clubs, babysitting

Table 1. My six month financial planner

Months	*Month one*		*Month two*		*Month three*	
Expected costs v. actual	*Expected*	*Actual*	*Expected*	*Actual*	*Expected*	*Actual*
Income:						
Net salaries						
Other						
Income total						
Outgoings:						
Transport						
Household						
Food						
Insurance						
Home & garden						
Holidays						
Social						
Dependents						
Personal						
Miscellaneous						
New baby						
Childcare						
Outgoings Total						
Bank opening balance						
Bank closing balance						

Months	*Month four*		*Month five*		*Month six*	
Expected costs v. actual	*Expected*	*Actual*	*Expected*	*Actual*	*Expected*	*Actual*
Income:						
Net salaries						
Other						
Income total						
Outgoings:						
Transport						
Household						
Food						
Insurance						
Home & garden						
Holidays						
Social						
Dependents						
Personal						
Miscellaneous						
New baby						
Childcare						
Outgoings Total						
Bank opening balance						
Bank closing balance						

My financial planning

In the space below, write some notes about what you discovered from your financial planning over six months.

Were there any surprises (good or bad!)?
Were there areas where you thought you were going to spend much more (or less) than you actually did?
Where were the biggest outgoings?
Over the next six months to a year, what changes might you want to make?
What long term savings plans for your children do you want to include, if any?

Notes:

Financial hints and tips

Look for simple ways to save money.

Try to get into the habit of planning your budget over a period of time in the way you did on the previous page. It is a good idea to monitor this kind of plan on a regular basis.

There are hundreds of items of baby equipment, toys and gadgets available to buy and, particularly with a first baby, it can be tempting to get carried away and end up with a house full of unused items.

It is worth getting feedback and recommendations—particularly for high cost items—from friends and relatives who have had children, or from other sources. See the Useful Contacts section at the end of the book.

A good website for money saving tips is www.moneysavingexpert.com which covers a range of savings including utility bills, insurance, banking, credit cards, coupons, and managing finances.

The National Childbirth Trust (NCT) holds "nearly new sales" across the UK where secondhand clothing, equipment and toys can be bought for much less than the original purchase price. You can find out about nearly new sales through the NCT website, details of which can be found in the Useful Contacts section at the end of the book.

Activity 1.15: Think before you buy

Before buying something, ask yourself the following questions:

Is it necessary? Do I really need it?

Is it more important to spend money on this than on the other things I need to pay for?

What savings could I make in order to pay for it?

Speak to other parents for advice on what is essential to buy for your baby and what is an unnecessary expense.

Speak to an independent financial adviser from a reputable company.

Check with your local tax office or Citizens Advice Bureau to find out what tax credits and/or child benefits you are entitled to.

Find out if your employer offers childcare vouchers; these can be a tax efficient way to pay towards childcare costs.

If you have credit cards or loans, calculate how long it will take to pay off the debt and how much interest will be charged. If at all possible, reduce or stop using credit cards unless the interest rate is zero percent or you can afford to pay the balance on request. Try to get into the habit of clearing your credit card balance at the end of each month.

Use comparison sites on the internet to check for best deals on rates and charges for products and services.

Remember to budget for Christmas, birthdays and other incidental expenses.

Chapter summary

You should now have reflected on many issues relevant to your own life goals and several practical issues relevant for pregnancy. At this stage you may choose to have a child, you may already be pregnant or you may choose to not have a child.

Whatever situation you are in, the more you can take control of your life, the better you will feel about it.

We will now turn to Chapter Two, which deals with pregnancy.

CHAPTER TWO

Pregnancy

This section is designed to help you examine your situation and the information you will have collated about pregnancy. We intend for you to identify what is going on right now, prepare for the inevitable changes that will take place at home and at work, and take control of your situation.

We will explore ways of dealing with the new experience of being pregnant and help you manage all of the information which is available (in books and online) so that you can work out what is best for you and your situation. We don't intend to provide information as that is readily available (see Useful Websites section at the end of the book); rather, we aim to help you use what you already know and have learnt and apply it to your circumstances.

Looking after yourself or your pregnant partner

Women today tend to be fitter and healthier than in previous generations and more capable of having babies into their forties. There are some typical symptoms and changes that pregnant women (of all ages) may experience:

- tiredness
- nausea
- increase in metabolism (the rate you burn calories)
- increase in blood volume
- sensitivity to smells
- heightened emotions.

We suggest that you contact your midwife/doctor if you are worried about any of these symptoms or refer to the NCT website for advice.

Here are some things to think about based on medical research and advice:

Poor nutrition during the first trimester of pregnancy can result in a baby with lower birth weight, reduced head circumference, less than optimum brain development and increased blood pressure later in life.

The following nutritional requirements have been suggested by doctors in pregnancy:

Protein (60g a day)—generates new tissue for you and your baby
Folic acid—brain and spinal cord development of your baby
Essential fatty acids
Fruit and vegetables
Plenty of pure water each day.

Activity 2.1: Diet and pregnancy

Considering the advice above, what changes to your diet, if any, do you need to make to ensure you are getting the best nutrition for you and your baby?

Research suggests that plenty of sleep and moderate exercise are important during pregnancy for a healthy mum and baby. The benefits of exercise are that it:

energises you
encourages mobility and good circulation
promotes healthy weight gain
promotes good posture.

The benefits for the baby are:

- blood volume increases which encourages your baby's growth
- develops sensitivity to motion, vibration and different sounds

Activity 2.2: Exercise

Thinking about the benefits of exercise during pregnancy, what changes do you need to make, if any, to your lifestyle.

Make a list here:

Please note that we strongly suggest you discuss exercise with your doctor if you have had previous health problems or conceived via IVF.

Dealing with stress

Stress during pregnancy will not only affect you, but also your unborn child as stress can be transmitted to the placenta.

There are a wide variety of ways of managing and reducing the stress you experience. Effective techniques for managing stress include breathing techniques, visualisation, yoga, and pilates.

Identify what triggers stress in you and how you can manage it. Is it the situation or your response to the situation? Stress affects different people in different ways so it is important for you to identify what causes you stress and how you can either adapt your approach to it, or how you manage it.

Activity 2.3: Stress triggers

Think about techniques that would work for you and make a note of them here: how often can you manage this?

Stress trigger	*How to handle it or relaxation technique*	*When to do it*

Dealing with bad news

It is very difficult to find out that your pregnancy may not be able to continue or that your child may have a disability. You may wish to refer to the change curve section in Chapter One to help deal with, and help you to understand and process, your emotional responses.

The section "Useful contacts and websites" has details of where you could go for help and support. There is a great deal of information available as well as counselling or support groups to help you cope with the psychological and emotional consequences.

Multiple babies

No one is sure why people have multiple babies—sometimes it can be a dominant maternal gene (responsible for creating identical twins) whereas fraternal (dizygotic) twins can run in families or it might happen following fertility treatment.

The news can come as a surprise and you will need to consider practical issues, such as how you will manage, especially if you already have children; whether or not you will be able to continue work (and for how long); and how your pregnancy will be affected.

Things to consider—the pregnant woman:

may feel sicker
may need more rest
should do some exercise, but not too energetically
may need to pay extra attention to nutrition, for example
extra protein and fluids, vitamins, minerals, and iron.

Your midwife or doctor may want to monitor you more closely with extra scans and blood tests. The "Useful contacts and websites" section has some organisations that you may wish to contact.

Sex during pregnancy

Pregnancy affects sexual desire in different ways depending on the couple. Many women find that pregnancy makes them want sex more than they did before they became pregnant. This sex drive is caused by hormonal changes. For some women, newfound voluptuousness can play a role in making them feel sexier than ever. Other women may find that their sex drive comes in waves while pregnant. Some women lose interest in sex due to sickness or tiredness. Men may also change their interest in sex—the man may experience a decrease in libido, less desire for his pregnant partner or concern with the baby's presence, or their sexual interest in their partner may be the same as before the pregnancy. Often, men do not talk openly about their sexual problems during pregnancy and health professionals rarely ask if the expectant father is experiencing sexual problems during his partner's pregnancy.

It is advisable to take care during the first trimester if you have had bleeding, a previous miscarriage or conceived via IVF.

It is important to talk openly and honestly with your partner about how you both feel.

Activity 2.4: Sex during pregnancy

How is your pregnancy affecting your sexual desire?

How is it affecting your partner?
What are the consequences of this?
What do you need to say to each other?
What else can you do to improve, if necessary, your intimacy?

Antenatal classes

Most future parents find antenatal classes helpful. Not only do you gain information about pregnancy and birth, some places incorporate hospital visits so that you can be familiar with the ward before the birth. Classes are usually offered through your midwife or doctor or you can pay to attend private classes.

Activity 2.5: Antenatal classes

What do you want to get out of attending antenatal classes?

Your answers	*Your partner's answers*

Where can you find out details of recommended, local classes?

Compare your thoughts with your partner's and discuss with them what each of you wrote down.

Baby names

Deciding the name for your baby is a very personal choice. Some people decide on a name during pregnancy (and may or may not wish to inform other people); others wait until after the birth or have a shortlist of possibilities.

In selecting names some people want to select a popular name, others a more unusual one. Some want a name from a family member or of a film star or other celebrity. Some people consider whether the name may lead to bullying, as well as the initials which would result from their selection.

Activity 2.6: Choosing your baby's name

What factors will guide your choice of a name?
Do you want to incorporate a family name—either as a first or middle name?
How popular do you want the name to be?
What acronym will the initials be?
What are the implications for your child of the different names you are considering?

Religious/Spiritual considerations

The decision on religious or spiritual beliefs (that is, whether parents want to raise their children according to a particular faith, and whether both parents agree on this, especially if they are from different religious backgrounds) is a personal one and depending on the strength of your beliefs, may influence how you wish to raise your child.

Before having children it is recommended that you discuss with your partner how much of a part you want religion/spirituality to play in your child's upbringing.

Activity 2.7: Religious beliefs

What are your religious beliefs?
Do you and your partner share the same beliefs?
If not, what compromises do you need to agree on?
How much do you want religion or spirituality to be part of your child's upbringing?

Planning maternity/paternity leave

During your pregnancy (if you are a working mother) then, at some point, you will need to have a discussion with your boss about maternity leave, how much time you would like to have off, and plans for your return to work.

If you are a working father, you may wish to apply for paternity leave from your employer. Different companies have different policies. Some operate a legal minimum, others offer more generous arrangements.

We suggest that you refer to the website www.workingfamilies.org.uk for information on your rights to maternity/paternity leave.

Activity 2.8: Planning your maternity/paternity leave

Where can you find out information on your company's HR/maternity and paternity policy?
What internal network do you have within your company to discuss how these policies work in practice?
When do you want to have a discussion with your manager about your maternity/paternity leave?

What are the key messages you want to convey to them?
What strategies do you need to put in place for the handover of your work before you leave?
What support do you need at work during this time leading up to your maternity/paternity leave?

What is your "keeping in touch" strategy with your employer going to be whilst you are off?
Make a list of the key areas for discussion with your boss which covers the issues you need to clarify and/or negotiate:

Chapter summary

We have now covered a range of issues that have hopefully been relevant to you during pregnancy. We hope you are enjoying the journey so far and that you are feeling ready for the challenge of the Big Day.

CHAPTER THREE

Birth

You and your partner are probably feeling a mixture of excitement and fear now that you are facing the birth of your baby. In this section we will take you through a number of issues you may want to consider before, during, and after the birth.

We will examine how you feel about labour and birth and what you can do to try to have the birth that, ideally, you would like.

Where do you want to have your baby?

The birth of your baby is undoubtedly a key event in your life. You do need to plan what sort of birthing arrangements are best suited to your needs and preferences, bearing in mind what is available locally to you.

It is important to keep an open mind as things can change during the birth process and your medical needs as well as those of your baby also need to be taken into account.

There are three places to plan to have a baby:

At home
In hospital
In a birthing centre.

Activity 3.1: Choosing where to have your baby

What kind of birth would you ideally like?
What medical conditions or complications, if any, need to be taken into account?

What is the advice of the midwife/doctor? How do you feel about that advice?

What do you need to consider if choosing a home birth?

Once again discuss your answers with your partner.

Planning for the birth

During pregnancy you will take in a lot of information about childbirth much of which may not necessarily be helpful during the birth itself. If you understand what is happening to your body, and your baby, you will be better equipped to take control, and end up feeling more empowered.

Many births don't go according to plan. They take longer or shorter, or happen somewhere else, than planned. Health considerations mean changes also need to be made to the original plan.

Activity 3.2: Planning for your birth

What do you need to find out about birth to feel less daunted?
What do you need to do to take control?

What are the key requirements that you need to communicate to your partner and/or midwife about your baby's birth plans?
How will you feel if your child's birth doesn't go to plan?

Managing stress/pain during childbirth

> "Women are amazingly capable of coping with the pain of labour and childbirth—much more than they could ever imagine".
>
> —*Agnes Bamford & Anna Golawski*

When people are unprepared or have no idea about their capabilities, they panic and make changes immediately, something which creates emotional stress. It will help therefore if you keep calm and think ahead. However much one may have read about birth, it is perfectly normal to feel anxious or stressed about an unknown event.

It is worth being realistic about birth—it is not pain-free and what you need to aim for is to trust your instincts, and do your best. It may be stressful for the partner who is not giving birth to experience the worry and pain of their partner who is going through this process. Think about how you want to be involved and help your pregnant partner during the birth—it may be useful to discuss your expectations before the birth.

In preparation for your child's birth it is a good idea to think about how you normally relax in stressful situations and how you can apply those strategies to childbirth. You may also find it beneficial to refer back to your answers in the "knowing yourself" activity in Chapter One.

We suggest you consider developing a personal action plan to manage the stress you may be feeling:

Activity 3.3: Stress and pain during birth

The strategies which people use to manage stress include simple breathing techniques, visualization, using smells from comforting items, touch and listening to music.

What are the aspects of the birth which you think will cause you the most stress?
What can you do to control your stress? Are you the sort of person who responds well to sounds, thoughts, music, smells or touch, relaxation, meditation?
Who do you want to be with you during labour?

What can your partner do during the birth to support you?

Some suggested techniques for helping to manage pain during birth are:

focusing energy on what you can control
focusing on breathing techniques
focusing on positive thoughts/words/mantras
visualising your muscles/pushing
choosing a position—standing, sitting, lying down, kneeling, leaning, walking.

Considering the suggestions above, what do you feel will work well for you?

Drugs

The subject of pain-relieving drugs for labour will no doubt crop up during antenatal classes and form part of your birth plan.

People's views on whether to take drugs or not range from wanting to do everything as naturally as possible without any assistance to wanting everything that is on offer from the very first twinge.

There is no right or wrong answer—it is your labour pain and people have different thresholds of pain tolerance.

Activity 3.4: Drugs

When thinking of your birth plan and whether you wish to receive drugs or not it is worth considering the following:

What would you wish to try first? What is your view on drugs for pain relief during birth?
What are the alternatives?
How would you feel if you have to take drugs? For example that you have failed somehow?

Be prepared to make adjustments to your initial plan in light of the actual event and how things develop. You should not consider it a failure to deviate from the original plan; it is your pain, no-one else's and only you can judge how bad it is.

Bonding

> "The mother's heart is the child's schoolroom".
>
> —*Henry Ward Beecher*

Many mothers, although by no means all, experience a huge and overwhelming rush of love when they see their baby for the first time. If you don't bond with your baby immediately, that's ok.

The reasons for not immediately bonding can stem from birth trauma, having a premature baby, having an emergency delivery, as well as other factors which can leave you feeling shocked and unprepared, or stressed and exhausted.

Bonding is simply getting to know one another and the love will deepen over time. You will have the opportunity over the first few weeks to bond with your baby at bath times, feeding times, and when you are changing him. The bond will develop when you cuddle and gaze at him and he starts to respond to your voice. It is also important to create opportunities for both partners to bond with the baby. This is particularly true if one partner returns to work soon after the baby is born.

Do remember that bonding and attachment represent a long-term, life-long process, and is not something achieved as a one-off event. We will return to attachment in Chapter Four.

Activity 3.5: Bonding

> Write a list of the key ways and times you would like to bond with your baby?

How will you support your partner to bond with the baby?

Looking after siblings

Older siblings may experience insecurities and ask questions about the new arrival. They will need reassurance that they will still be as loved and wanted by their parents.

You can involve them by allowing them to feel the baby's movements in your tummy, or letting them talk to the baby.

Engaging and involving other family members—siblings, grandparents, close friends—so that they feel involved, will help the process. Try to plan in advance what help and support different people can offer. If you don't have extended family or close friends nearby, who else can you turn to for help and support?

Activity 3.6: Siblings

What support network will you need to look after other children when you go into labour or if you have to stay in hospital after the birth?

How will you help older siblings make the baby feel welcome in your family?
How can you help the older sibling feel included when attention is given to the new baby?

The more prepared and in control you feel, the less stressed and anxious you will feel which is better for you and better for baby.

It is important to plan when and how will you talk to, and prepare, the siblings for the new arrival. Listen to their concerns, fears, anxieties and hopes, and respond to their questions.

Breast or bottle?

There has been increasing awareness and substantial research over the last few years about the benefits of breastfeeding over bottle-feeding babies.

The health benefits of breastfeeding babies are well documented. Breastmilk:

- is naturally designed for your baby and contains all the nutrients your baby needs
- contains antibodies.
- is easily digested.

Furthermore, breastfed babies:

- are less likely to develop allergies such as eczema or asthma.
- are easier to wean.

Premature babies are more likely to do well on breastmilk than formula milk.

Even if you only breastfeed for a few weeks, your baby will receive the benefit. There are also added benefits for mum:

pregnancy fat is used up and helps the woman get back into shape quicker (though she should not diet whilst breastfeeding).
Breastfeeding helps her womb to contract and return to its normal size.
Breastfeeding is practical—especially in the middle of the night!

However, some mothers are not comfortable with, or able to, breastfeed. Bottle-feeding is a satisfactory alternative which allows partners and others to share the task, thus enabling greater flexibility (including permitting the mother to sleep) and quantity of food intake to be monitored.

It is important not to feel guilty when you choose to bottle-feed, given the many advantages of breastfeeding that are publicised. The experience of the child being cuddled and held close is important in either method.

Activity 3.7: Feeding

For your own situation, what do you consider the advantages and disadvantages of breastfeeding and bottle-feeding to be?

	Breastfeeding	*Bottle-feeding*
Advantages		
Disadvantages		

Given these factors, how long do you consider you may wish to breastfeed?

If things don't go to plan, where can you turn to for support and advice?

Chapter summary

We have now covered many issues that you may want to think of leading up to, during, and after the birth of your child. You have been through a transformational change—you now have a new person in your life. You are likely to experience a range of emotions, something which is perfectly normal. And we will begin the next section by looking at "the culture shock" of having a baby.

CHAPTER FOUR

The first year of your child's life

As new parents we spend a great deal of time choosing what kind of birth we would like. We are also likely to spend some time gathering information about practical day-to-day issues such as feeding, bathing, nappy-changing, sleeping etc., and adapting our lives to such changes. We are less likely to spend time reflecting on the emotional changes we are going through following a birth and the introduction of our child into our world. Whether we like to admit it or not, having a baby (especially the first one) can seem like a culture shock, and it is perfectly normal to experience a roller-coaster of emotions, from the euphoria of being infatuated with your new baby to feeling very low due to lack of sleep. When you consider all these feelings to be normal, you are more likely to feel in control and content.

Having a baby: a culture shock

Having a baby represents a fundamental change in your life and it is very common to experience it as a form of culture shock in the midst of the happiness of being a parent.

Adjusting to having a baby is similar to other new changes in our lives.

It is normal to experience this as a series of ups and downs, usually experienced by any change, but it is more intense for new parents.

The height and depth of the ups and downs vary as well as the length at each stage. The new mother and father will often be at different stages at any given time.

Activity 4.1: Signs of culture shock

Signs of culture shock: what are you experiencing?
Please mark all that apply:

__ Fatigue
__ Loss of sense of humour
__ Tension and conflict with your partner (family)
__ Withdrawal
__ Loss of identity
__ Under/overeating
__ Increase of illness or accidents
__ Crying—sense of sadness
__ Sense of isolation
__ Inability to concentrate or work effectively
__ Excessive need for sleep or not being able to sleep.

The adjustment process

Graph showing the ups and downs of the adjustment process

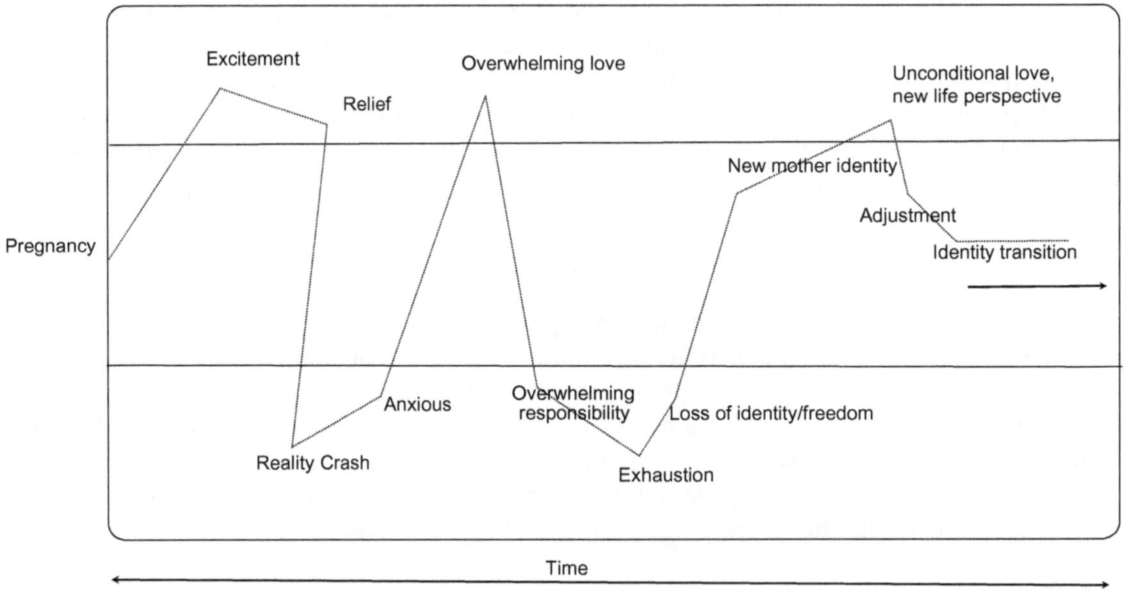

The graph shows the following phases:

Stage	*Interpretation*
Pregnancy	The status quo: your pregnancy is underway and the next key milestone is the birth.
Excitement/relief	This stage is categorised by feelings of excitement around your new arrival. You may feel overwhelmed with the news after your arrival, you may feel excited. You may feel relieved if this is a long-awaited pregnancy, a long/complicated labour, or just relieved to meet your new baby.
Reality crash	Some people may feel a "reality crash" after the initial excitement has worn off and the sleepless nights/hormones have started to kick in. This may occur in the first few days or weeks, if indeed it happens at all. Awareness that this is part of the natural process can help individuals deal with the emotions and make plans for the future. It is important at this stage not to compare yourself to unrealistic images portrayed in the media/advertising and to accept that you are doing your best in the circumstances and learning every day.
Overwhelming love	With a newborn baby, there is often a feeling of overwhelming love and joy. This may be felt immediately after the birth, or after a few days or weeks. The timing and intensity of the feeling will vary from person to person.
Overwhelming responsibility	Often coupled with overwhelming love, there is the conflicting emotion of overwhelming responsibility for your newborn baby and the realisation of your role as a parent. This stage will vary according to the person's situation. For many people it shows that theyhave begun to accept the reality of being a parent and the lifestyle changes that will need to be made.
Exhaustion	This phase can be characterised by feeling exhausted physically and emotionally. The level of exhaustion will vary according to the duration of the labour, the type of birth, the support network around the parents, and how soon the mother returns to work. It is important at this stage to look after yourself and your baby; you may find it useful to reflect on the needs of children as discussed earlier in the book.

Loss of identity/freedom	Again, this stage varies according to the person's situation, although broadly it is an indication that there is some clarity around the circumstances and objectivity. At this stage, you are likely to make decisions about your lifestyle and how having a baby is going to change your current situation. It is at this point that you may want to start to put in place some plans.
New parent identity	At this stage you will be feeling more confident in your role as a parent. The initial overwhelming feelings will have largely faded and you may notice you are feeling "yourself" again and enjoying the responsibility of being a parent.
Unconditional love/new life perspective	This stage is characterised by feeling more confident in your role as a parent and enjoying feelings of unconditional love for your baby, and with a lessening of the earlier fears and anxieties. Sometimes this stage is coupled with thoughts of returning to work and a reconsideration of the values you have in relation to your career. The timing of this stage will vary for parents depending on their situation.
Adjustment	Again, this stage varies according to the person's situation, although broadly it is an indication that there is some clarity around the circumstances and objectivity. You may be in a familiar routine or pattern with your baby. At this stage, you are likely to make decisions about your lifestyle and how having a baby is going to change your current situation. It is around this time that you might start to devise some plans, particularly those concerning returning to work.

It is not uncommon for new mothers to experience a degree of post-natal depression. If the symptoms are severe or persistent, it is important that advice is sought from your GP.

Similarly, some women suffer severe and prolonged symptoms related to the trauma of giving birth, sometimes related to complications during labour and birth. In such cases effective help is available and women need not feel embarrassed or hesitant about seeking advice and help from their GP.

Activity 4.2: Swings and roundabouts

Where are you now in the process?
What behaviour, thoughts and feelings will indicate that you have really adjusted to becoming a parent?
How can you help yourself adjust to the new situation in order to make it as enjoyable as possible?

We will now look at the new roles you and your partner will take on to deal with some of the changes to your family life.

Roles—who will take on which roles? (will this change over time)

> "There are no mistakes, only lessons".
>
> —*Chinese proverb*

As the mother usually spends more time with the new baby during the first few weeks the role of a partners often becomes more traditional, even for couples who are strongly committed to gender equality and are used to sharing household tasks. Mothers spend more time in close proximity to the baby, especially if breastfeeding.

This can be difficult for new mothers who have been used to an active involvement in a career. It can also be hard for fathers, who may feel left out by the special bond which they see being formed between mother and baby, and from which they are excluded. This may cause feelings of loss, and even depression, in new fathers. Research shows that the larger the difference in men's and women's responsibilities, the greater the rise in conflict and decline in the couple's happiness and mental health following childbirth, especially for women. Violated expectations about jointly caring for a new baby contribute to the decline in the couple's happiness. Women, especially, count on far more help from their partner than they usually get.

When negotiating expectations it is important that the parents talk, communicate well, and accept a process of give and take. Examples of areas of parental life which may need some negotiation includes feeding, sleeping, bedtimes, routines, clothes, and arrangements. Parents need time to sit down and discuss their joint approach.

Activity 4.3: Roles

Who will be the main carer for the baby in the beginning?

How will you deal with your changing roles?

How and when do you plan to review what happens after the first few weeks/months?

How does this feel for the father?

How could the father's role and needs be specifically considered?
What steps should be taken now, and in the near future?
What does father need? How could these needs be met? What plans need to be put in place, e.g., some time for the father for activities on his own

Dealing with a crying baby

Crying is the most important mechanism newborn babies have to communicate with the world. Babies have several different types of cries, of which the most common are:

The basic cry: a rhythmic pattern which is thought to be generated by hunger.
The anger cry: a variation of the basic cry, this cry is associated with exasperation or rage and involves excess air being forced through vocal chords.
The pain cry: this differs from other types of cry being characterised by the sudden occurrence of loud crying without initial moaning and a long cry followed by the baby holding its breath.

Most parents and adults can determine whether a baby's cry indicates anger or pain and parents can distinguish the cry of their own baby better than those of a stranger's baby (Santrock, 2010).

"What to expect: the first year" (Murkoff, Eisenberg & Hathaway, 2009) is one of the many books advising parents on how to deal with crying babies.

Our coaching approach means that we encourage you to think about and to talk about your responses to a crying baby. We believe parents usually know their baby best and thus have a good sense of what to do and when.

You may at first need to adopt a trial and error process of finding out what a particular cry means, through responding in different ways to see if that helps, for example feeding, winding, holding, showing the baby new shapes and objects, or putting on music and making sounds that you know the baby likes.. Our babies are very good teachers if we listen carefully to their language!

You can get further advice on this and other topics on the popular parent websites which are listed in the "Useful contacts and websites" section.

Activity 4.4: Crying

If you find that your baby is crying more than expected how will you deal with this?

Where can you get support or help during these times?
How will you manage conflicting advice which comes from family, friends and perhaps professionals?

Dealing with night-time disturbances

All babies wake up during the night at different stages, and most manage to fall back to sleep on their own after the age of six months. Unfortunately, this is not something you can teach your child to do, but rather is something they must learn by themselves. And the only way they will learn is if you give your baby the chance to do so. This means encouraging your baby to find her own ways of getting back to sleep when she wakes up crying at night, and letting her, as far as possible, settle on her own without your help. This may take time.

As far as possible, it is best to avoid overstimulation at night, while at the same time avoiding extreme distress, or the baby crying for long periods.

Parents, particularly the ones who spend much time with their child, are the experts and should trust their instincts, these being very strong. An experimental approach allows things to be tried, particularly with crying, feeding and sleeping. We need to learn from our own baby. Parenting is an interactive process.

Activity 4.5: Night-times

Who will get up in the night if the baby cries?
How will the other partner/family members support the person who is getting up?
In what room will the baby sleep?

Developing attachment

> "We cannot fashion our children after our desires, we must have them and love them as God has given them to us".
>
> —*Johann Wolfgang von Goethe*

We now wish to return to the issue of bonding/attachment which we briefly touched upon in the Birth section.

Attachment can be described as a close emotional bond between a baby and parent (carer). It is the strong, affectional tie we feel for special people in our lives that leads us to feel pleasure and joy when we interact with them and to be comforted by their nearness during times of stress (Berk, 2008). By the second half of the first year, infants have become attached to familiar people who have responded to their needs for physical care and stimulation. Watch your baby and notice how you have become singled out for special attention. A whole range of responses are reserved for you as parents; when the mother or father enters the room, the baby breaks into a broad, friendly smile. When you pick up the baby they pat your face, explore your hair and snuggle against your body. When they feel anxious they crawl towards you or stay close.

According to Bowlby, (1982) the infant's relationship to the parent begins as a set of innate signals that call the adult to the baby's side. Over time, a true affectional bond develops. This is supported by new emotional and cognitive capacities as well as a history of warm, sensitive care. The development of attachment takes place generally in four phases.

Phase 1: Birth to 2 months:	Babies instinctively direct their attachment to anyone.
Phase 2: 2 to 7 months:	Attachment becomes focused on the main carer, as the baby gradually learns to distinguish between familiar and unfamiliar people.
Phase 3: 7 to 24 months:	Babies actively seek contact with regular carers, such as the parents and specific attachment develops.
Phase 4: 24 months onwards:	Children become aware of others' feelings and understand language and begin to understand more why parents are coming and going and can predict their return, so accept being separated (Santrock, 2004).

According to Bowlby (1982), from their experience during these four phases, children construct an enduring affectional tie to the caregiver that permits them to use the attachment figure as a secure base across time and distance. This gives the child expectations about the availability of people they are close to and their likelihood of providing support during times of stress. The image becomes a guide for all future close relationships, through childhood, adolescence and into adult life.

Containment, reciprocity, and attunement

There are at least three important attachment processes which are very important in developing future healthy and positive relationships. (Garland, (1998); Brazelton et al., (1974); Cameron, (2011); Douglas, (2007)). These are known as:

- containment
- reciprocity
- attunement.

Containment is a process whereby the parent is able to pick up on and grasp their baby's anxieties, and manages to stay calm and in control without getting overwhelmed or distressed themselves. This gives the baby a strong feeling of safety.

Reciprocity is the ability to share feelings, worries, and concerns experienced by the baby; the ability to "dance together" and share feelings. This process, when working effectively, enables the baby to feel safe and understood.

Attunement is the process of understanding the very special language, signals and communication, mainly non-verbal, of course, emitted by the baby—his or her special distinct language. If your baby is called Bertie, for example, then you really have to learn to understand Bertie-ese very quickly!

Activity 4.6: Containment, reciprocity, and attunement

1. How far are you able to recognise these ideas in your communication with your baby?
2. Could you deepen even further your communication with your baby, along the lines of the above containment, reciprocity, and attunement processes?
3. Talk about these processes with your partner, friend or others.
4. What are their views about how you communicate and relate to your baby through the lens of containment, reciprocity, and attunement?

Activity 4.7: Attachment

How would you describe your baby's attachment to you at present?
What have you learnt about attachment that will impact you as a parent?
Given your answer to the above, what would you like to do more or less of to further build your relationship with your baby?

Separation

When we have developed a close bond to our baby, it may be painful for both the parent and child to separate from one another. Most babies will cry when they are left with someone other than their main carers; this is called separation anxiety (Santrock, 2004) and tends to occur around 6 months after birth and may last until the child is eighteen months to two years old. However, even if you are caring full time for your baby, there will be times when you will have to leave them with someone else.

Separation experiences are best if they are gradual, careful, sensitively planned, and made up of very small steps, starting from, for example, a child being in a different room from a parent for just a few minutes.

Activity 4.8: Separation anxiety

Bearing in mind attachment and separation anxiety, when do you think is the ideal age to leave your child with others or in childcare?
How can this be graduated?
What type of childcare would you choose as a result of being aware of the importance of attachment?

Children's needs

Dr Mia Kellmer-Pringle, former Director of the National Children's Bureau, identified the main developmental needs of children (1986). Her work is considered to be a landmark in our understanding of childhood. Kellmer-Pringle claimed the following four needs have to be met in equal quantities:

The need for love and security

The need for love is met when children experience a stable, continuous, dependable, and loving relationship with the adults who love the children and whom they love from birth. These relationships form the basis for children's self-worth, healthy personal development, and their future relationships with others; they also serve as a basis for their ability to respond to affection and, in time, to become a loving, caring parent themselves.

The need for security is mainly met by giving the child the security of stable family relationships where attitudes and behaviour are consistent and dependable; the security of familiar places and known routines. If the whole framework for children's lives is secure, it provides them with the needed reassurance to venture out into life as they know they can return to safety.

We now appreciate the vital and immense importance of touch, tactile experiences, and cuddling for children's emotional development.

The need for new experiences

New experiences are a prerequisite for intellectual and cognitive growth. From birth onwards, the child's mastery of tasks appropriate to each stage of development provides stepping stones towards more difficult achievements, for example from having learnt to grasp and hold an object children proceed to feed themselves. If denied the opportunity of having new experiences, no learning can take place. For example, children will have to experience a language spoken around them in order to acquire speech, otherwise they will not learn to speak even though their hearing and speech organs are normally developed.

An excellent book on how babies think is called *How Babies Think: The Science of Childhood* by Alison Gopnik, Andrew Meltzoff, and Patricia Kuhl (2001).

The need for praise and recognition

Growing from a helpless baby into a self-reliant adult requires an extensive amount of emotional, social, and intellectual learning, and strong incentives are needed to overcome difficulties and setbacks. Praise for success provides such an incentive when given by the adults who love the children and whom the children love and want to please in return. An optimal level of expectation needs to be geared towards capabilities at a given point in time and stage of growth, at a level where success is possible but not without effort (we will return to praise in section 5).

The need for responsibility

This need is met by allowing children to achieve independence. At first this is achieved by children learning to take care of themselves by feeding, dressing, and washing themselves; and then gradually extending the responsibility to other areas, including imitating what their role models (parents) do. It makes sense to offer maximum help at first and gradually to allow the child to do more and more for herself, all the while praising the child for any signs of progress, however small. Despite the challenge of giving responsibility to immature and irresponsible children, children can only learn about exercising responsibility by being given the chance to practise this themselves, gradually and systematically.

It is also important to add that many psychologists would note the need for consistency, structures and reliable routine (Docking, 1987).

We return to responsibility in Chapter Five.

Activity 4.9: Children's needs

Reflect on Mia Kellmer-Pringle's four developmental needs. You may like to review how you are meeting the needs of your baby under these four headings:

Needs of children	*How are you meeting these needs?*	*What else could you do to meet these needs?*
Love and security		
New experiences		
Praise & recognition		
Responsibility		

Adults also have these needs, and we could equally categorise these under similar headings.

How are you meeting your partner's needs or supporting friends/family?
How are you making sure your own needs are met?
How are you providing consistency, structure, and routine for yourself/your family?

Milestones

> "We find delight in the beauty and happiness of children that makes the heart too big for the body".
>
> —*Ralph Waldo Emerson*

Throughout your child's life there are going to be many milestones. Some of these are causes for celebration, while some are just part of childhood development.

In the spirit of this coaching book, we are deliberately not going to outline when a child should be walking, talking, weaned, or potty-trained, as all children are unique and individual and develop in their own time.

It is not helpful or constructive to compare baby stages at the parent and toddler groups, as it is far better to understand your own child and how they develop and what you can do to encourage them. For example, a daughter of one of the authors of this book was considered very late in walking but when she was ready she got going in her own time and walked confidently rather than tottering baby steps. The same pattern of development has been observed with potty training, reading and writing.

Indeed, with spoken language, it can seem that the child is not making much progress at all, and then there is a sudden " growth spurt" showing that, all the while, your baby has been taking in lots of ideas, words, and language, and much learning has been going on internally. When the spurt happens, we can become surprised at the sudden jump in speaking that we notice.

However, if you do have cause for concern about your child, then please ask your health visitor or doctor for advice.

A number of children will inevitably have special needs or significant difficulties of some kind at some point during their lives. They may then require more help with their progress and learning than is arranged for children without such individual needs. Fortunately, there are many agencies that can assist, including those in the education, health and social care services of your local authority; the help that they may be able to offer could involve specialists such as advisory teachers, educational psychologists, speech and language therapists, occupational therapists, paediatricians, and others. Most professionals believe that their early involvement is beneficial. Again, if you have any concerns about your child's future educational or developmental needs during the first year, it is wise to speak with your doctor about your child.

Weaning

The current advice is that babies should be weaned from milk and liquids to solid food at around 6 months. The point at which a baby is weaned will vary from child to child and the key factors to consider are signs of hunger in your baby (demanding feeds more often or waking in the night for feeds after sleeping through) and their weight; bigger birth weight babies (4+ kg) tend to start needing solid foods earlier.

A good place to start is to discuss weaning with your health visitor.

It is important to note that babies should continue to have milk alongside the introduction of solids.

The reasons for weaning babies are to satisfy their appetite, to gradually introduce them to a variety of tastes and textures, and to provide more iron and nutrients than milk alone can provide.

All babies are different and, as parents, you need to feel confident about what you are doing for your children and not feel pressurised by others asking you about weaning stages. Eating should become an enjoyable and social aspect of your baby's life.

However, prepare yourself for mess! This is a totally new experience for you and your baby, so have a large bib and plenty of wipes to hand.

Some babies are hungry and take to solids immediately, while others may take a few weeks; so do not feel pressurised into comparing yourself to others as it is far more important to set up a long-lasting, positive, stress-free attitude towards food for you and your baby.

For details on suggested food for weaning and further information, please refer to the useful contacts section at the end of the book.

Remember that your baby is a unique individual, progressing at his or her own pace, and expressing his or her own needs. Professional advice will help you arrive at effective decisions. However, it is a good idea to experiment and try different approaches to find out which work best for you and your baby.

The development of language and thinking

The development of language, communication, and thinking skills are vital for your baby's future educational and intellectual development. In the first year, relatively simply activities and behaviours such as your baby's showing an interest, watching, looking and gazing, playing and exploring (even if through the mouth) as well as his making minimal responses are in fact the foundations for future learning, communication, understanding, and language.

Babies often begin simply by attending to objects and people, smiling and laughing at specific events, and are thus learning about shapes and movement and, of course, people. Cooing and babbling are early forms of communication and experimentation with sound (Macintyre, 2012).

The first word is a major event, and one which often occurs towards the end of the first year, but there is significant individual variation. In the second year, we can expect an increase in word vocabulary, and then gradually little sentences, starting with two word patterns and gaining in complexity.

Although we know that language and communication development is affected by the interaction of nature and nurture, there is no doubt that our responses as adults make a huge difference. Babies understand much more than they can express, and their understanding or comprehension of things may well surprise us, even from a few days or weeks old (Gopnik et al., 1999).

Language, thinking, and communication can be encouraged by adult praise, attention and modelling and, for example, by the adult asking questions and explaining things—even if the words seems to be ahead of the child's current understanding. A lot goes in, and children learn from repetition, songs, voice patterns, and the song of language. They learn from pictures, toys, and play as well as the way in which adults speak to them—for example, with careful explanations, giving them time and taking trouble to explain things. They learn from outings, seeing new things, experiencing new events and, of course, listening to stories and songs. Children are naturally curious; the way that we, as adults, encourage this, or perhaps fail to stimulate this capacity, may make a big difference for the child's future learning.

We know that language development is a vital foundation of future thinking, learning, and understanding and later on reading and general progress at school … and life. We also know that what happens at this very earliest stage of the child's life makes a critical impact. Think of how hard it is to learn a foreign language as an adult compared to when one is younger (Gopnik et al., 1999).

Thus, the importance of our focus on, and encouragement of, this area of the child's development at an early stage cannot be over-emphasised.

You can read more about this in an excellent book by Alison Gopnik, Andrew Meltzoff, and Patricia Kuhl (2001) called *How Babies Think: The Science of Childhood*.

Although children's rate of progress in the areas of language and communication is very individual, and later than average development should not necessarily cause alarm, if parents do become concerned about their child having speech or learning difficulties or seeming not to respond, then advice should be sought from the GP in the first instance.

Activity 4.10: Language development

Thinking of your baby's language, communication and thinking skills (in the broadest sense), what can your child do at this stage?
What do they seem to like or respond especially well to?
How do they respond to: words stories music and songs toys and playing different people?
What could you do to further encourage your baby's language, communication, thinking skills, and general development (e.g., taking more time to explain things, modelling, reading or telling stories, singing, playing, praising)?

Maintaining your relationship with your partner

Having a baby may split open any hairline fractures in your relationship. The initial euphoria and excitement of having a new baby can lead to a shocking bump back to reality.

As mentioned earlier, the early weeks after a new baby enters the family are full of profound changes (see "culture shock" at the beginning of Chapter Four). These include disrupted sleep schedules, less time for the new mother and father to devote to each other, and new financial responsibilities. A combination of these factors may lead to a decline in a couple's happiness. This may not happen immediately, but may build up during the first six months. It is important to recognise negative feelings at the outset and to be open about these with your partner. In accepting negative feelings you are more likely to be able to deal with them.

Spend some time together in these early days to explore how you are feeling as a new mother and new father.

Activity 4.11: Your relationship with your partner

How has your relationship changed?
What do you find difficult in the new situation?

What do you enjoy about the new situation and what can you celebrate?
What do you love about your new baby? What is unique and special about him/her?

Letting your feelings be known

It's important that you make your feelings known as this will have a positive impact on how you go forward as a couple and how close you will remain in years to come.

When you're in the midst of tiredness and trying to just get through the day, you may not have the energy to focus on how your partner is feeling.

As a new parent you may want to let your partner know that you think (s)he is doing a terrific job, whilst you remind him/her that you also need regular doses of tender loving care.

As a new parent you may not realise that as you are getting to know the baby you may be losing touch with your partner.

As a new parent, you may want to discuss with your partner how the two of you can remain close in spite of the new situation.

Activity 4.12: Letting your feelings be known

How can you create special time for yourself?
How can you manage your expectations in the new situation and minimise conflict?
How do you (will you) let your partner (family/friends) know that you appreciate their help and support?

Finding special time for yourself

In the first few months of a baby's life, when the demands of feeding and caring for your baby round the clock are seemingly endless, all you may have the time and inclination to crave is sleep. Once the baby has settled into a routine, and parents have established a manageable rhythm, the frenetic fog of the early days may begin to lift, especially for the parent looking after the baby (assuming you are not both back at work). If you were involved in many activities before—a career, hobbies, school, sport, community activities, etc.—you may start feeling that you are now ready to resume some of these activities, gently and gradually. However, as a new father or mother, you may start doubting your self-worth as well as your decision to stay home with your baby.

Yet a rich, full, satisfying lifestyle and life with baby can be combined and enjoyed. The important first step toward rediscovering your former confidence and achieving such a lifestyle is to recognise that woman and man cannot live by baby alone. Even if you adore every moment with your baby, you still need intellectual stimulation and the chance to communicate with someone with whom you can have an adult conversation. There are a variety of ways of achieving these goals, and of reclaiming the sense of self you feel you've lost.

Activity 4.13: Getting out and about

What activities exist for babies in your local area?
What interests do you have that you can take your baby to?
What activities can you attend for your own enjoyment if your partner, family, friends or others can look after your baby?

Finding time for romance

The period of new parenthood is one during which it is easy for couples to grow apart instead of getting closer. Yet your relationship with your partner is the most significant in your life. It was your love for each other that created your family in the first place, and it is that love that can best nurture and sustain your relationship with each other.

Nevertheless, the relationship with your partner is very easily taken for granted. If you neglect your relationship, the results are often not apparent at first; but they can erode a relationship before the partners even realise it.

Think of how you can continue to invest in your relationship with your partner (or family and friends). Spending some quality time together each week is crucial.

Activity 4.14: Quality time with your partner

Think of at least three ways you can connect with your partner (family/friends) each week that do not involve going out or hiring a babysitter and list them below:

1
2
3

When can you arrange to meet with your partner to have a quiet and uninterrupted time to discuss managing your child's behaviour and agreeing expectations on how to raise your child?

New mothers: getting your body back

Although pregnancy-stretched muscles regain some of their tone as time goes by, they won't ever return to their pre-pregnancy condition without a concerted exercise effort. Exercising after birth will do more good than simply pulling your tummy in. Abdominal routines are known to improve general circulation and reduce the risk of back problems, varicose veins, and leg cramps. Perineal exercises will help you avoid stress incontinence (which sometimes occurs after childbirth), dropping (or prolapse) of the pelvic organs and will tighten your perineum so that making love, once you resume it, will be as good or better than ever. Regular exercise will also promote healing of your battered uterine, abdominal, and pelvic muscles, hastening their return to normal and preventing further weakening from inactivity. Exercise is also known to improve your ability to handle stress and to relax, while reducing the risk of postnatal depression.

Activity 4.15: Getting your body back

What kind of exercise do you enjoy most?
How can you include exercising into your daily routine with your baby?
How can you plan some time for exercising by yourself as part of your wider weekly routine?

Work/Life balance

Returning to work

Maternity and paternity leave often coincides with a key point on the career ladder and the main decisions to make (after the financial necessity about returning to work) are about whether to return and pick up your career where you left off or whether you want to "hold back" for a while whilst managing work and a family. It is important to consider your values, ambitions, and feelings towards work and career so that you can effectively plan your return to work.

Many parents return to work at some point during the baby's first year and this is when the term "work/life balance" really comes into its own! As well as getting yourself ready for work, you also have a baby to get ready and often have to add a detour onto your journey to work to take them to childcare.

Getting the balance right between work and family is unique for each person so it is important that you identify your career ambitions and family ideals and think about where you see yourself in the future.

Some thoughts that parents have around returning to work after maternity/paternity leave include:

How will I fit back into the organisation?
How will I be perceived by my manager/peers?
How will I cope with the juggling demands of work and family?
Will I be able to do my job effectively?

Activity 4.16: Work/life balance

Should I go back to my old job or a new one? If so, when?
How much income do I need to cover living expenses—can I do this working part time? (you may wish to refer to the financial planning activity in Chapter One)

What are the additional childcare costs that I need to cover whilst working?
Aside from financial considerations, what satisfaction do you also hope to achieve from work—socially and intellectually?
What are your employer's options for part-time or flexible working?
What support network do I have around me (partner, friends, family) that can help if I'm late back from work or if my baby is unwell?

Taking stock of your career to date and reflecting on your key highlights and successes will help you make informed career decisions, boost your confidence and self-esteem. You will be in a better position to speak to your boss about your ideal role when you return.

It is worth re-visiting the "managing maternity/paternity leave" activity that we did in the pregnancy chapter and thinking about how well the maternity/paternity leave went, how good the communication was during the time off work, and preparing for returning to work. Are there any changes or actions that you need to take?

If returning to employment, make a list of the key areas for discussion, clarification and negotiation with your boss. If you will be self-employed, what issues do you need to plan and organise?

Activity 4.17: Managing maternity/paternity leave and returning to work

Question	*Thoughts and any changes required.*
How often do I want to keep in touch with my boss during maternity/paternity leave?	
What would be effective communication for both of us?	
How can I re-connect with stakeholders when I return?	
What would my ideal future work pattern look like?	
How do I want to re-integrate myself into the company?	
What are my boundaries?	
With whom do I have key relationships at work?	
How do I need to manage those relationships?	
What is my definition of success?	

Consider carefully what is most important in your life. List your values and needs in order and put them down on paper. They may include your baby, your family, your career, financial security, material wealth, holidays, study—and may be totally different from the person next door or from the list you wrote at the start of the workbook when you were expecting your baby. After writing down your priorities, consider whether returning to employment or staying at home will best meet the most important of your needs and values.

Activity 4.18: Where am I now?

(Repeat Activity 1.1 for your current life situation)

Where are you now (in your life) with regards to work, social life, your relationship?
Where do you want to be?
How do you want to be as a parent?
How often will you review these priorities?
How will you ensure you stay on track and achieve what you have planned?

Managing finances when returning to work

Below we have included the six-month financial planner from section 1.

How will you manage your finances with additional childcare and other costs factored in?

Activity 4.19: My six-month financial planner

Months						
Budget v. Actual	*Budget*	*Actual*	*Budget*	*Actual*	*Budget*	*Actual*
Income						
Net salaries						
Other						
Income total						
Outgoings						
Mortgage/rent						
Loans/HP/Credit						
Household						
Insurance						
Transport						
Garden						
Food						
Holidays						
Social						
Dependents						
Personal						
Mobile phone						
Other						
Childcare costs						
Outgoings Total						
Bank opening balance						
Bank closing balance						

Months						
Budget v. Actual	*Budget*	*Actual*	*Budget*	*Actual*	*Budget*	*Actual*
Income						
Net salaries						
Other						
Income total						
Outgoings						
Mortgage/rent						
Loans/HP/Credit						
Household						
Insurance						
Transport						
Garden						
Food						
Holidays						
Social						
Dependents						
Personal						
Mobile phone						
Other						
Childcare costs						
Outgoings Total						
Bank opening balance						
Bank closing balance						

Choosing childcare

Your values and awareness of what is good for your child will affect your choice of childcare. In addition, your choice of childcare is linked to what childcare options are available where you are, whether you are a full-time parent, working part-time or full-time, as well as financial considerations, including how much money you are willing to spend on childcare, how big your home is, and whether you welcome someone to come and live with you.

It is also important for you to consider how you feel about having help with looking after your children and how you can balance it with your image of yourself. How do you feel about being an employer of someone looking after your children?

The most common childcare options in the UK are:

live-in nanny (full- or part-time)
live-in mother's help or au pair (full- or part-time)
daily nanny (full- or part-time)
nanny-share (full- or part-time)
registered childminder (full- or part-time)
private or state day nursery (full- or part-time)
crèche at work
babysitter
kinship care provided by grandparents.

To help you navigate your way through the jungle of different options, which might seem quite daunting at first, consider the following questions.

Activity 4.20: Choosing childcare

Do you want your child looked after in your home or elsewhere?

If you want your child to be looked after in your home, do you want the carer to live with you or to come to the house every day?

What might be the implications of your decision for you and your family?

Are your working hours compatible with your choice of childcare?

What are your top criteria in choosing care for your child?

Do you want your child to be looked after individually or together with other children? If so, how many?

Many parents feel that it is best for their child to be looked after in his own home surrounded by his toys, that he can nap in his own bed, play in his own garden and have his own friends round for tea.

Other parents feel less strongly about this and like their child being with other children while they are out at work, provided that the children have plenty of stimulation and activities. In this case, they may feel that taking the child out of his own environment is fine.

If you are happy to let your child be looked after outside of their home, do you prefer that they have a particular person looking after them each day, such as a childminder, or would you like them to attend nursery?

Option	*Advantages*	*Disadvantages*

For more information see "The Good Childcare Guide" in our references and website sections, which explains the different childcare options in detail.

Reflections on being a parent

Read the following poem of parenthood –and reflect on how the situations and feelings described relate to you as a mother or father.

Before I was a parent

Author unknown

Before I was a Parent
I made and ate hot meals
I had unstained clothing
I had quiet conversations on the phone

Before I was a Parent
I slept as late as I wanted
And never worried about how late I got into bed
I brushed my hair and my teeth everyday

Before I was Parent
I cleaned my house each day
I never tripped over toys or forgot words of lullabies

Before I was a Parent
I didn't worry whether or not my plants were poisonous
I never thought about immunizations

Before I was a Parent
I had never been puked on
Pooped on
Spat on
Chewed on
Peed on
Or pinched by tiny fingers

Before I was a Parent
I had complete control of:
  My thoughts
  My body
  And my mind
I slept all night

Before I was a Parent
I never held down a screaming child
So that doctors could do tests
Or give shots
I never looked into teary eyes and cried
I never got gloriously happy over a simple grin
I never sat up late hours at night watching a baby sleep

Before I was a Parent
I never held a sleeping baby
just because I didn't want to put it down
I never felt my heart break into a million pieces
When I couldn't stop the hurt
I never knew that something so small
Could affect my life so much
I never knew that I could love someone so much
I never knew I would love being a Parent

Before I was a Parent
I didn't know
the feeling of having my heart outside my body
I didn't know how special it could feel to feed a hungry baby
I didn't know that bond between a Parent and child
I didn't know that something so small
Could make me feel so important

Before I was a Parent
I had never gotten up in the middle of the night every 10 minutes to make sure all was okay

I had never known the warmth
The joy
The love
The heartache
The wonder

Or the satisfaction of being a Parent
I didn't know I was capable of feeling so much
before I was a Parent

Activity 4.21: Reflections on being a parent

What situations and feelings in the poem above can you relate to as a new parent?
What has changed in your life since having a baby?
How have you changed?

How has your partner changed?
What kind of change did you expect?
What was unexpected?

Chapter summary

In this chapter we have covered a range of practical issues to consider as a new parent, as well as child development and the needs of both parents and children. In the next chapter we will focus on more practical and emotional issues in the parent-child relationship as well as inviting you to reflect more on who you want to be as a parent.

CHAPTER FIVE

Next steps

> "Creating a warm, caring, supportive, encouraging environment is probably the most important thing you can do for your family".
>
> —*Stephen R. Covey*

You have managed to get through the first year as a parent. Congratulations! In this section we will cover practical issues you will have to deal with as a parent, different types of feelings and behaviour you and your child may be experiencing, and invite you to reflect on how you can create a great relationship with your child in the future. We also invite you both to reflect on your role as a parent and to ensure that you take care of yourself. We will furthermore ask you to imagine what the world looks like from your child's perspective.

How will you manage household tasks?

Activity 5.1: Your role as a parent

What do you think/feel about how you are managing household tasks?

How has having a child changed the way you share/manage household tasks?
How can you communicate constructively with your partner and find a way to manage the tasks that suits you both?
What ideas do you have about fairness and expectations of how to share these tasks?
Thinking about your child's longer-term future (that is, when they have grown up), what are your big hopes, dreams, and wishes for their development? (Whatever they are, start right away, even if slowly and gradually, leaving plenty of scope for the children to make their own choices)

For a humorous take on what is involved in being a parent, please take a look at a "Job description for parents" on the following page.

Parent job description

Long-term player needed for challenging, permanent work in chaotic environment. Candidates must possess excellent communication and organisational skills and be willing to work evenings, weekends, and frequent 24-hour shifts. There is some overnight travel required, including trips to primitive camping sites on rainy weekends and endless sports tournaments in far-away cities. Travel expenses not reimbursed.

Responsibilities: Must keep this job for the rest of your life. Must be willing to be hated, at least temporarily. Must be willing to bite tongue repeatedly. Must possess the physical stamina of a pack mule. Must be willing to tackle stimulating technical challenges such as small gadget repair, sluggish toilets, and stuck zippers. Must handle assembly and product safety testing, as well as floor maintenance and janitorial work. Must screen phone calls, maintain calendars, and coordinate production of multiple homework projects. Must have ability to plan and organise social gatherings for clients of all ages and levels of mental aptitude. Must be willing to be indispensable one minute and an embarrassment the next. Must assume final, complete accountability for the quality of end product.

Advancement and promotion: There is no possibility of either. Your job is to remain in the same position for years, without complaining, constantly retraining and updating your skills so that those in your charge can ultimately surpass you.

Previous experience: None required, but on-the-job training is offered on a continually exhausting basis.

Wages: None. In fact, you must pay those in your charge, offering frequent raises and bonuses. A balloon payment is due when they turn eighteen and attend college. When you die, you give them whatever income you have left.

Benefits: There is no health nor dental insurance, no pension, no tuition reimbursement, no paid holidays, and no stock options. However, the job offers limitless opportunities for personal growth and free hugs for life.

What sort of parent do you want to be?

> "We never know the love of a parent till we become parents ourselves".
>
> —*Henry Ward Beecher*

Being a parent is one of the most challenging and rewarding roles you will experience in your life. No other life experience is likely to leave you with such a range of emotions, including joy, anger, happiness, frustration, pride, embarrassment, sadness, elation, despair, and love. No parent seems to feel that they are completely in control or feel that they are great parents. Most of us are quick to point out our shortcomings instead and tend to focus on problems or issues we find difficult about being a parent. You may want to revisit the three archetypical parenting styles in Chapter Two—both to reflect on how you wish to parent and on how you were parented yourself.

Activity 5.2: Parenting audit

How do you regard yourself as a parent?
How can you get more enjoyment out of your family life?

Even though your children are young at present it is worth starting to think about your aims as a parent for the long-term.

What are your hopes and aims as a parent?

What kind of relationship would you like to have with your children when they are grown up?
How do you want to lay the foundations for this relationship right now?

If you want your children to have a close, open, and honest relationship with you in the future (when they will have important decisions to make) it is important you lay the foundations now.

Think about the communication you have with your children; is it open and honest, does it involve careful, sensitive, and appreciative listening based upon the child's perspective?

Do they tell you what they feel and think and experience?

Do you tell them enough how gifted they are, what their special skills are, or how well they are doing?

When are you able to give them your full attention to listen (even to what may appear to be trivial to you!)?

Have you noticed a time when they open up and want to talk? Some parents notice that bath-time or bedtime is when their children are most talkative (although some may think it's a stalling tactic for a later bedtime, it's usually because that is when they have full parental attention with no distractions)

What levels of trust are you building up for your children so that they know they can confide in you?

What reassurances (verbal and nonverbal) do you give them?

How much fun and laughter do you have now?

How can you enjoy more things in life together with them to build happy memories for the future?

What is your relationship with your parents like?

Sometimes we have to become parents ourselves in order to understand our own parents and what they may have been through when we were children. As parents we are generally excellent at criticising ourselves and telling ourselves and others what we are not doing well and should be doing better. What we say about ourselves has tremendous power, positively and negatively. Unfortunately many parents are constantly reinforcing an image of themselves as parents who just don't come up to scratch. Remember that if this is what you're doing, you are providing a negative model for your children. So by changing the way you see yourself, you will be able to help your children be more positive in themselves and allow them to build valuable, positive self-belief.

The good news is that the majority of challenges are within our control and, if we commit to dealing with them, we can deal with them effectively. Don't be put off if the problems currently seem too big to deal with. Break them down into small steps so that you can easily handle them and instead spend your time focusing on enjoying life with your children. Remember, we are all human and no-one is perfect.

Activity 5.3: Your relationship with your parents

Think about the relationship you have with your parents.
What do you admire most about your parents?
What do you enjoy/value most about the relationship with your parents you have as an adult?
What did you enjoy/value most about your parents when you were a child?
What changes happened in the relationship with your parents, from your childhood to adulthood? What were the consequences of that?
Would you do anything differently?

What has worked well with your parents?
What would you like to replicate for your own children?
What mistakes will you choose to avoid?

Focus on the qualities and strengths that make you the great parent that you are.

To help you with this, please answer the questions below. It will be very beneficial if you discuss the answers with your partner.

What three values are most important to you as a parent? 1) 2) 3)
What are your three most significant achievements as a parent? 1) 2) 3)

What is the greatest challenge you have overcome as a parent?

What three things do you love most about being a parent?

1)

2)

3)

What three things do you love most about your child(ren)?

1)

2)

3)

How has being a parent helped you grow as a person?

What three personal qualities make you a good parent?

1)

2)

3)

What three skills make you a good family problem-solver? 1) 2) 3)
If you could tell your child(ren) about the biggest positive difference they have made to your life, what would you say to them?

Sometimes the chaos of family life means that we focus on the negatives rather than the positives. It's easy to focus on the challenges and lose touch with what makes us passionate and happy about being parents.

Activity 5.4: Thought patterns

Spend the rest of today saying only positive things about yourself. Really focus on your positive qualities and achievements as a parent and the love and passion you feel.

What difference does it make to how you feel when you say only positive things about yourself?

> "The journey of a thousand miles starts with a single step".
>
> —*Mao Zedong*

Noticing your thoughts

Notice how your thoughts affect you. Make a note of some of the unexpected good/wonderful things that happen when you decide to be in a positive state of mind.

Make a note of the thoughts that get you into a good mood.

1)

2)

3)

We appreciate it is not easy to monitor your thoughts, especially in the heat of the moment, but if you saw the value in it, you may be tempted to do it more often and even make a habit of it.

Remember that you are in control of your thoughts, your feelings and your behaviour, and therefore your actions.

Establishing a good frame of mind and moving forward positively

As a parent you have lots of juggling to do, but if you want to help develop your child and enjoy the journey, you must be in the right frame of mind. Take a fresh look at your life.

Activity 5.5: Take a fresh look

Step 1

Get into an energised positive frame of mind. Think about activities that make you feel good and do them for a few minutes.

Some examples are:

Take a brisk walk
Play some music and sing along to it
Stand up and have a big stretch
Jump up and down ten times
Stand outside and take some deep breaths of fresh air
Dance

Step 2

Start noticing what you do well with your children. Go one step further and make a list to keep near you as a reminder. This can provide a great boost to your confidence and self-esteem which can really help you to push through barriers and move you towards being the parent you want to be. So, are you ready to make a commitment to yourself and start creating a life that you love?

What I do well:

1)

2)

3)

4)

5)

6)

7)

8)

Step 3

Eliminate the word "failure" from your vocabulary—it can be quite a liberating experience! Start thinking of failure as just a different outcome or result to what you had expected, as errors rather than failures. Thus, an error is simply an opportunity to learn and modify things!

Some of your greatest learning will come from these different outcomes, so don't deny or ignore them. Rather, celebrate the experience and the learning you have gained. Also, make a note of what's good in your life right now. We can sometimes be so focused on what's not good that not only can we miss valuable opportunities, but we miss the good stuff that is happening around us too!

What's good in my life right now?

Step 4

This "wheel of life" exercise will help you to put some priorities in order and also to look closely at your life at the moment.

Wheel of life

NAME: ________________________________ DATE: ____________________

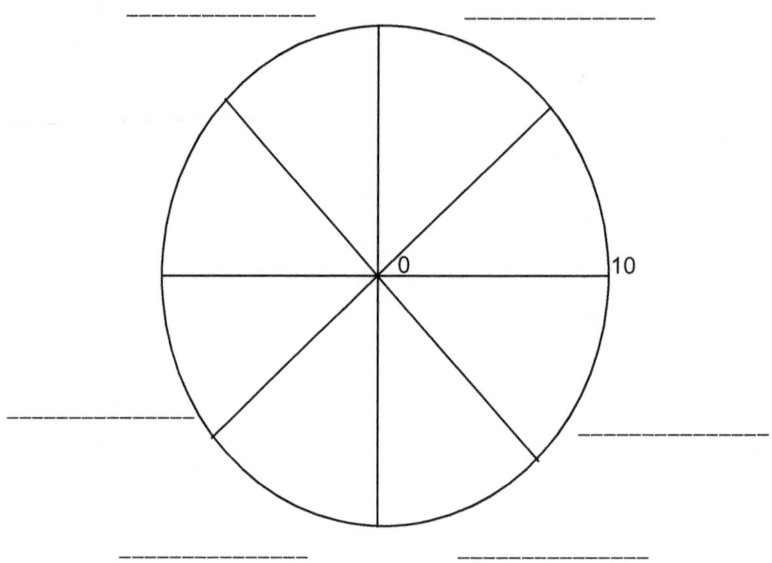

Example

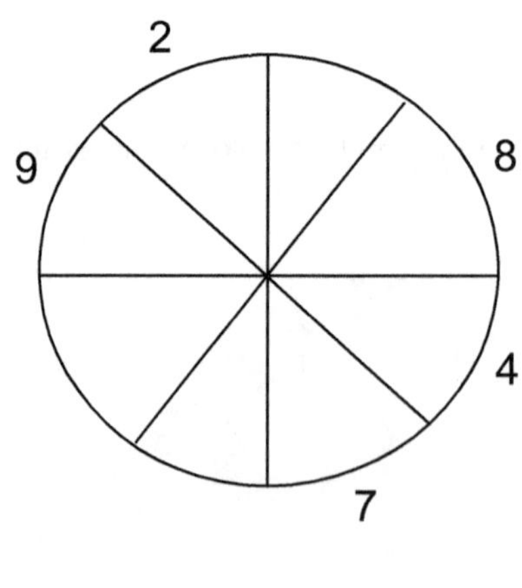

Wheel of life instructions

The eight sections in the Wheel of Life represent aspects of your life. Please change, split or rename any category so that it's meaningful for you.

Next, taking the centre of the wheel as 0 and the outer edge as 10, rank your level of satisfaction with each area out of 10 by drawing a straight or curved line to create a new outer edge (see example).

The new perimeter of the circle represents your "Wheel of life".

In the centre of the section of the wheel below, write eight areas of your life that are most important to you. For example money, health and vitality, physical environment, friends, partner, fun, recreation, personal development/growth, quality time with partner, social life, etc.

What three areas can you add to your wheel that relate to your children and you as a parent?

Give each section a score between 1 and 10 as to how you feel about that part of your life right now. For instance 1 is the lowest and might be rated "catastrophic" and 10 is the highest and might be rated as "fantastic".

For example Business—6; Money—2; Family—5; Partner—2; Health—6; Fun—3; Social life—2.

In the middle section of the wheel write one thing that would greatly enhance this particular area. Think about what would make it a 10. Or if you have a score of 10 already, what would make it even better?

For example:

Partner—spend more time together
Health—do more regular exercise

In the outer section of the wheel write one thing that you could do right now that would improve this area of your life. For example:

Partner—invite them for an evening with you when the TV is off
Health—commit to going swimming with a friend

Step 5

Dream time!

Spend at least twenty minutes thinking about and filling in the following section. Let your imagination run away with you and write down everything according to your wildest dreams. Assume no limits of time, money or age.

Everything I want to do

Everything I want to have
Everything I want to be

Step 6

What's most important?
Pick the six things you want most from these three lists and write them down below (do not worry about order or priority).

Under each "want" briefly write how, if you had it now, it could improve your life.

Want	*How it will improve my life*
1	
2	
3	
4	
5	
6	

Step 7

What's important?
Transfer your "want" list to the following worksheet and, referring back to your wheel of life, ask yourself if you had this "want" how would it improve the individual sections of your life.

For each section that you consider it will improve your life, give it a point in the score box. Repeat this exercise for wants 2–6. Finally, count up the scores for each of the chosen six wants.

You may find that 2 or 3 score the same, or there may be one thing that's way above everything else. Focusing your attention and effort on the highest scoring topics will have the greatest positive impact on your life as a whole and is a great place to start making some changes!

Wants score total

1)

2)

3)

4)

5)

6)

Choose one area to work on initially, and then you need to create goals that are specific, measurable, achievable, realistic, and tangible/timely (SMART).

Focus on two goals you can achieve in the next week.

Goal 1

I will..

Start date..

How I will track my progress...

What support I will need ....

What will be the benefits of doing this? For myself:...

For others?...

Goal 2

I will..

Start date..

How I will track my progress...

What support I will need ....

What will be the benefits of doing this? For myself:...

For others?...

Having had an opportunity to reflect on who you are and who you want to be as a parent we will now concentrate on how to generate a constructive and enjoyable relationship with your child(ren). We also explore important factors to consider for your child's healthy development, such as language development, play, praise, setting boundaries, dealing with emotions, communication, labels, choices, and responsibility.

The importance of play

We know that play is fundamental to learning; it is how children learn about the world, have new experiences, develop communication and language skills, develop social and interpersonal skills, learn about relationships, ideas, science, experimentation, objects and how things work. Play is a vital part of early development.

Even from birth, babies interact playfully with others and are learning about relationships from day one. From the age of two, children begin engaging in play more obviously with others. There is a dramatic increase with age in joint, interactive play. Social development seems to proceed in a three-step sequence. It begins with unoccupied, onlooker behaviour and solitary play. Then it shifts to a form of limited social participation called parallel play, in which a child plays near other children with similar toys etc. but doesn't try to influence the others' behaviour. At a higher level children engage in two forms of true social play; associative play (engaging in separate activities, but they interact by exchanging toys and commenting about each other's behaviour and cooperative play in which children orient toward a common goal such as acting out a make-believe theme or working on the same activity, for example a castle or painting). All these types of play co-exist during the pre-school years. Furthermore, although non-social activity declines with age, it is still the most frequent form of behaviour among 3- to 4-year olds (Berk, 2008).

Activity 5.6: Play

What type of play does your child engage in?
What imaginary games do they play?
How can you support your child's development through play?

Praise and sanctions

Children's behaviour is subject to processes of learning, and we know that it is shaped by consequences, rewards, praise, and sanctions.

Praise is one of the fundamental needs of children, as mentioned in Section 4.

The kind of praise that is joyful and springs from the heart gives our children what they need most: our genuine loving support.

Helpful praise can be divided into two phases, according to Faber & Mazlish (2001).

1. The adult describes with appreciation what they see and feel, being as specific as they can be.
2. The child, after hearing the description, is then able to praise herself.

The more specific the praise the child receives from the adult, the more appreciative and aware the child becomes of her own strengths, as demonstrated in the following examples:

> "You made me a card with animals and farm-houses and trees and a tractor. You have used green and red and blue—great colours. I really love the card. Thank you".
>
> "You sorted out your pencils, crayons, and pens and put them in separate boxes. You are so organised. It's a pleasure to walk into this room".
>
> Psychologists have suggested that we should give praise at least five times as often as we criticise or give negative feedback or criticism (Kline, 1998).

One method that is often helpful in getting the balance correct has been termed the Positive—Negative—Positive Sandwich. Using this method, if the parent has commented negatively on, or criticised, some aspect of behaviour, it is best to begin with something the child has done well, then make the criticism with a clear statement of what is needed to be done to improve, and then end up with a positive remark. For example, one might say, "it was really nice how you made that drawing today, but you do need to put fruit peel in the bin rather than on the floor. You have been working really hard at keeping your room tidy".

It is also important to avoid "ego attacks" whereby one comments about the child rather than the behaviour. For example, one should avoid general ego attacking statements such as "you are a naughty boy" and refer directly and specifically to the behaviour which the parent wishes to modify and praise.

Psychologists also often distinguish between "extrinsic" and "intrinsic rewards" whereby children are given rewards after positive or "good" behaviour. These can be tokens, stars, money, toys etc. (extrinsic rewards) or the enjoyment of doing the activity itself (intrinsic rewards). The latter tend to come later on in the child's development. There are myriad websites which provide examples of star charts, reward certificates, and other plans and ideas to help parents and children with programmes to reinforce good behaviour. Most last for a few weeks before attracting a degree of boredom but, by that time, significant improvements have been made and the heat can be taken out of what might otherwise be a tense interaction between adult and child.

Sometimes it will be necessary to sanction children, and the evidence suggests that any sanction needs to be immediate, minimal, related to the misbehaviour and time-limited. For example, two minutes sitting in a quiet area, or losing the use of a toy for five minutes, can be an effective sanction, rather than a prolonged one or an emotional threat (though it should go without saying that emotional threats should never be used).

Activity 5.7: Praise

What would you like to praise your child for? What would you like to praise yourself for?
How can you role model praise?
What sanctions would you consider, and under what conditions?

Sometimes people find it hard to give praise. For some people it can be easier to write what we mean to say rather than say it out loud.

It is important to separate praise from love. Children need unconditional love, not love that depends upon what they do. It is therefore helpful to praise and criticise *behaviour* rather than the child himself. One can always say, explicitly, "mummy loves you, but did not like [such and such] behaviour", thereby making this distinction clear.

It is also worth bearing in mind that you can use the Positive—Negative—Positive sandwich with your child, children or other adults. It works for all of us!

Activity 5.8: A letter of praise

Write a letter to your children. Tell them what you love about them. If you wanted them to remember what you thought about them, forever, what would you say about them and the difference that they have made to your life?

Communicating with our children; listening

Listening is something that we do automatically—and sometimes unintentionally—with very little conscious effort. However, it is important that you, as a parent, listen effectively to your children to really hear and understand what they are saying and meaning. This type of listening involves concentration and a great deal of skill.

Listening to babies and young children requires focus and effort. It requires observing, watching, and becoming attuned to your child.

> "Deal with the fault of others as gently as your own".
>
> —*Chinese proverb*

The hardest and most vital part of great listening is to concentrate on what the other person is saying, as opposed to thinking about what you are going to say, forming an opinion or being distracted by what is going on around you. You can allow distractions to come and go without paying much attention to them, just notice that you have got distracted and focus on what you were listening to before (The Mindgym, 2009).

Parsloe (1995) outlines three types of listening:

Peripheral—this takes place at a subconscious level and requires no effort as it entails picking up snippets of other people's conversations.
Apparent—this is what we do the majority of the time and, although we hear what someone is saying, we are not concentrating or analysing what is being said.
Active—this is where we concentrate on what is being said and why.

Some psychologists stress the importance of what is termed "appreciative listening" where we listen carefully to the other person's side of the story, their perspective and feelings, in a supportive way, asking questions to understand, and taking a stance which communicates respect, understanding, and being on their side.

Activity 5.9: Communication

Try to imagine what the world seems like to your children or indeed your partner.

> Reflect on how you listen to your children and your partner. How can you improve your listening?

Activity 5.10: Listening

Next time you sit down with your partner or children, listen to them actively. Try to be open to what they have to say without making judgments. Listen with interest and respect, allowing them time to express themselves without interruption.

What difference did this make for how you connected with your partner and children?
What difference do you think it made to your partner and children being listened to like this?

Dealing with our own and our children's feelings

There is often a direct link between how we (and our children) feel and how we behave. When children feel good, they behave well. So how do we help them (and ourselves) to feel good? We can start by accepting their (and our) feelings. One problem is that we often don't recognise our own feelings and the effect these have on our behaviour; nor do we accept our children's feelings. Steady denial of feelings can confuse and annoy children. It also teaches them to be confused about what their feelings are, and perhaps not to trust them. What may help is to start recognising our own feelings (see the activity below) and to put ourselves in our children's shoes. Imagine being a child who was tired or hot or upset, and suppose you wanted that all-important adult in your life to know what you were feeling … As parents we can start by recognising that we are separate people to our children, and as such we and they are capable of having two sets of feelings. For example, they may be feeling hot, even though we are cold; or hungry, even though we are not. We can start by accepting that there are no right or wrong feelings.

What makes it difficult to recognise our own and others' feelings is that many of us grew up not talking about our feelings and probably had our feelings denied (Faber & Mazlish, 2001).

Activity 5.11: Dealing with feelings

What are your various needs and feelings at present? (list both positive and negative ones)
How do we learn to name and deal with these feelings?
How do, for example, feeling irritated or happy influence the way we parent?
Think about your children …
What different needs and feelings do they have?
How do your children learn to name and deal with these feelings?

Activity 5.12: Helping your children deal with their feelings

How can you discover, respect, and accept your children's feelings?
How can you help them express their feelings?

For more information on dealing with feelings see Faber & Mazlis (2001).

> "The best way to make children good is to make them happy".
>
> —*Oscar Wilde*

Approaches to discipline and children's behaviour

> "If you want your children to improve, let them overhear the nice things you say about them to others".
>
> —*Haim Ginott*

A child's behaviour is a response to the circumstances that pertain at the time, and which may have built up over time, including external and internal factors. External factors may be separation from parents, being in a new place or sibling conflict, whilst internal factors may be teething, insufficient sleep or developing illness.

Although we know there are many causes of misbehaviour, we may choose to see them as isolated from what may have brought it about.

A crucial question to ask is if this is misbehaviour or just behaviour we don't like.

"Misbehaviour" can be viewed as a good learning opportunity for us to teach children new, more appropriate ways of behaving, using praise to encourage the behaviour we wish to see more of.

When a child has a tantrum we need to think about the effect our own response is having—are we helping the situation by acknowledging the child's feelings or do we simply respond with our own frustration?

A tantrum is a signal of helplessness and fear, even though it may give the opposite impression: that the child is trying to be more powerful than we are. The best approach is to express empathy while validating the child's feelings: "Oh dear, your brother knocked over your great tower again! How frustrating!"

Other successful ways to discipline a child include pointing out to a child a way they can be helpful instead of criticising them, expressing strong disapproval without attacking their character, stating your expectations clearly, giving children a choice, and allowing them to experience the consequences of their misbehaviour.

The hardest part of making this work is to shift our attitude away from thinking of the child as a "problem" that needs correction. It requires a change of perspective to believe that if we take the time to engage with our child and share our real feelings with them and listen to their feelings that, together, we will come up with solutions that will be right for both of us. For more information on dealing with misbehaviour see Faber & Mazlish (2001); and if you are interesting in finding out about a great technique for disciplining children, see Phelan (2000).

> "Never judge a person unless you have walked a mile in their shoes".
>
> —*Sioux proverb*

Activity 5.13: Discipline

What is your child doing that you would consider misbehaviour? What could be going on for your child?

Robert Dilts (1988) developed the meta-mirror, a way of understanding someones else's perspective and the positive intent behind their behaviour, which enable you to manage a situation much more objectively. The meta-mirror works by getting us to observe what's going on from three different perspectives.

Imagine that your child is behaving in a way you don't like. Now, let's look at the situation from three perspectives:

1. Our own
2. Our child's
3. The objective observer.

1. In this first phase you explore your own view of the situation. Imagine the situation and picture your child there with you.
   What do you see, hear and feel? Immerse yourself in the situation. Now describe what you are doing—are you shouting or listening? What's your body posture? What are you saying?

At this moment, what are you honestly thinking and feeling about your child's behaviour? And what about them as a person? And what would you most like to say to them? What do you think your child is feeling about you?

Now you are going to look at the world through your child's eyes.

Think about the physical characteristics of your child: how does he walk? With what speed, volume, and tone does he speak? Think about the language he uses to express himself.

Now play the episode again from the start, but this time you are acting as your child. Keeping as close as you can to his physicality, notice how you react to the situation. Explore the feelings, intentions, and hopes that you experience as your child. Notice the tactics that you use.

Ask yourself these questions:

What do you see, hear, and feel?

What do you notice about the parent (that is, the person who is you in the real world)?

At this moment, what are you thinking and feeling about their behaviour? And about them as a parent? And what would you most like to say to them?

And what do you think your parent is thinking about you?

2. In phase three we become an impartial and wise observer. In order to do this we imagine ourselves as an independent, concerned, and very intelligent fly on the wall that has seen a million scenes just like this and given wise advice on many occasions on how to increase understanding and empathy. In this role, replay the scenario in your head so that you can see and hear both the parent and the child as if you were standing next to them. Then answer the following questions:

   Based on what you are seeing, what is each person thinking? And feeling?
   What advice would you give the parent in order to understand the child better?
   What would you advise the parent to say or do differently in order to show greater empathy and build a stronger relationship?

3. Now we step back to you—the parent. Take a look at the answers and see what insights there are about how the child is feeling. How can you use these to understand the child better and build a stronger connection between you and her? (Mindgym, 2009).

How can we teach our children more appropriate behaviour?

We know that consistency and modelling are important. Children need clear, reliable structures and consistency. They also learn through modelling and observing parental behaviour, and that of significant people around them, including siblings.

How can we ensure consistency, structure, and routine in our management of behaviour?
What behaviour might we be modelling for our child? How can we use modelling to help our child learn desirable behaviour?

Choices and consequences

It is helpful for children to gradually learn how to make choices, and to discover what happens as a result of the choices they make. If they aren't given the chance to learn this, they may grow up knowing only how to do as they're told, which is of little help when it comes to adult life, or they will make choices without realising they are making them, and fail to take responsibility for them.

If children are given no choice, they will feel powerless, which usually brings with it a host of other difficult feelings , and results in behaviour which is difficult for the children themselves, and for those around them, to manage. We may want to strike a balance between giving no choice and giving too much (Hunt, 2009).

Activity 5.14: Choices and consequences

A plan for trying out choices and consequences:

...., you have a choice (child's name)

You can either...
(positive behaviour choice)

or you can ....
(negative behaviour choice)

If you choose ....
(positive behaviour)

then...
(positive consequence)

If you choose ....
(negative behaviour)

then...
(negative consequence)

It's up to you—it's your choice.

Using the formula for giving choices and consequences can sometimes seem to take more time than laying down the law. However, in the long-term it's much quicker, because you don't spend so much time arguing and sorting out all the resentment that builds up when children feel powerless.

Giving children responsibility

> "Tell me, and I'll forget.
> Show me, and I may remember.
> Involve me, and I will understand".
>
> —*Chinese proverb*

As mentioned previously, responsibility is a fundamental developmental need for children. Children need to be allowed to do things for themselves, wrestle with their own problems, and learn from their own mistakes. Whilst you help them learn these skills you are also giving them a sense of responsibility and they become more confident in their abilities. We can encourage our children to take responsibility by letting them make choices: "Do you want to wear the red top or the blue top today?"

We can show respect for a child's struggle: "A jar can be hard to open. Sometimes it helps if you tap the side of the lid with a spoon" (Faber & Mazlish, 2001).

Encouraging responsibility can be quite complicated for parents. As much as we understand the importance of our children being independent, there are forces within us that may work against it. Most of us are busy and in a hurry, which means that we may do everyday tasks for our children as it seems so much faster to do it for them. We also have to fight against the feeling of wanting to protect our children from all harm in the world and instead gradually let them go. It's also hard for parents not to give advice, particularly when we're sure we have the answers and instead let them learn to solve problems themselves.

We also have to take into account the importance and pleasure we get from being needed as parents. It's a road of paradoxes we parents travel. We start with total commitment to a small, helpless baby. Over the years we worry, plan, comfort, and try to understand. We give our love, labour, knowledge, and experience—so that, one day, they will have the inner strength and confidence to leave us. And we have to learn how to attach and then let go.

Activity 5.15: Responsibility

What tasks can you encourage your children to do that will encourage their sense of themselves as independent people?
How will you make this happen?
What are you doing for your child at present that your child might start doing for himself?
How can you shift this responsibility to your child without him feeling overwhelmed?

The labels our children wear

We may all agree that labelling of children or other people is unconstructive. However, sometimes all it takes is for a few words, a look, or a tone of voice to tell you that you're either "slow or stupid" or a "likeable and capable" person. How we as parents think of our children can be communicated in seconds. When we multiply the seconds by the hours and years of daily contact between parents and children we begin to realise how powerfully young people can be influenced by the way their parents and other authority figures view them. Both children's feelings about themselves and their behaviour is affected by this.

Even though a child has been cast into a role for whatever reason, he does not have to play it for the rest of his life—he can free himself from the labels.

When we want to free our children from negative labels they may have put on themselves we can show children new pictures of themselves.

We can put the children in situations where they see themselves differently. We can let children overhear that we say something positive about them—praise them to other family members. We can model the behaviour we would like to see in the children (Faber & Mazlish, 2001).

Activity 5.16: Labels

What labels might your child have been given, either at home, school, by friends or relatives?
Is there anything positive about the labels?
How would you like your children to think of themselves?

It may be useful to think about our long-term aims, hopes, and dreams for our child(ren) even if that seems remote.

Thinking ahead, many parents say that their aspirations are for their child to:

be happy
be healthy
be safe
gain increasing self-confidence and independence
become socially skilled
be emotionally well-balanced
get on well with people, and help others
do their best at school
do the best they can do in all areas of their lives
be resilient
be able to cope with adversity
be able to solve problems for themselves
enjoy a balanced life, including an enjoyment and appreciation of different spheres of life such as the arts, music, sports, leisure time, hobbies, and spiritual matters
express themselves as unique and wonderful individual people.

You may wish to add your own here........

What are your personal aims, aspirations, dreams, and hopes for your child? What can you do, even at this early stage, and using the smallest of steps, to promote these aims for your child?

As Kahlil Gibran (1998) reminds us, so beautifully:

> " Your children are not your children. They are the sons and daughters of Life's longing for itself. They come through you, but not from you and though they are with you, yet they belong not to you".

Ready to do it all again?

At some point after having your first baby, you may start thinking about having another baby. There is no right or wrong age gap and the ideal number of children and years between them is a very personal decision.

Activity 5.17: Ready to have another baby?

Coaching questions to consider are:

What do you feel having another baby would add to your life?
How would having another child affect your lifestyle and routine?
What adjustments may you have to make? At home and work?
Would you need additional support? Where might you get this from?

Chapter summary

In this chapter we have reflected on who we are and want to be as parents and we have looked at our own relationship with our parents. We have also focused on important issues in children's development and the parent-child relationship.

We have now come to the end of "Swings and Roundabouts". We hope you have enjoyed the journey with us and wish you the best of luck on your ongoing journey as parents—a journey that will continue for the rest of your life. We very much welcome feedback—so please feel free to contact us via the email addresses below.

WHERE TO FIND HELP

The authors of this book offer parent and maternity coaching for schools, individuals, and businesses via group workshops or on a one-to-one basis.

This can be for individual parents wishing to have personal coaching, for schools looking to improve the relationship between the school, parents, and pupils, or for forward-thinking companies who wish to support their working parents and enable them to be more engaged and productive at work whilst feeling fulfilled and confident at home.

If you are interested in finding out more, please email:

Anna Golawski at Stratus Coaching: anna@stratuscoaching.co.uk

Agnes Bamford: agnesmariebamford@yahoo.co.uk

Professor Irvine Gersch: I.Gersch@uel.ac.uk

Coach training at The University of East London

The University of East London is one of the leading providers of coach training, consultancy and research in the UK.

The University provides short courses, post-graduate training, research, and advice for individuals and organisations.

FURTHER READING AND REFERENCES

Berk, L. (2008). *Child development. 8th ed.* Massachusetts: Allyn & Bacon.

Biddulph, S. (1998). *The Secret of Happy Children.* London: Harper Collins.

Biddulph, S. (1999). *More Secrets of Happy Children.* London: Harper Collins.

Bowlby, J. (1969a). *Attachment.* London: Pimlico.

Bowlby, J. (1969b). *Attachment and Loss. Volume 1: Attachment.* London: Penguin Books.

Bowlby, J. (1979). *The Making and Breaking of Affectional Bonds.* London: Routledge.

Bowlby, J. (1980). *Attachment and Loss: Volume III. Loss, Sadness and Depression.* London: Hogarth Press.

Bowlby, J. (1982). *Attachment.* London: Hogarth Press.

Brazelton, T. B., Koslowski, B. & Main, M. (1974). *The Origins of Reciprocity: The Early Mother-Infant Interaction.* In Lewis, M. & Rosenblum, L., (Eds) *The Effect of the Infant on it Caregiver.* London: Wiley.

Cameron, R. J. (2011). Personal Communication.

Covey, S. (1998). *7 Habits of highly effective families.* London: Simon & Schuster UK Ltd.

Dilts, R. B. (1994). *Strategies of Genius.* California: Meta Publications.

Docking, J. W. (1987). *Control and Discipline in Schools: perspectives and approaches.* London: Harper and Row.

Douglas, H. (2007). *Containment and Reciprocity.* Hove: Routledge.

Faber, A. & Mazlish, E. (1999). *Siblings without rivalry.* London: Piccadilly Press.

Faber, A. & Mazlish, E. (2001). *How to talk so kids will listen, and listen so kids will talk.* London: Piccadilly Press.

Garland, C. (1998). *Issues in Treatment: a case of rape.* In Garland, C. (ed) Understanding Trauma: a psychoanalytical approach. London: Duckworth.

Giles, S. (2006). *You're the Daddy.* London: White Ladder Press.

Goodhart, K. (2008). The good childcare guide: *The complete handbook on nannies, Mother's helps, aupairs, childminders, day nurseries, After school care and maternity nurses. Richmond*: Crimson Publishing.

Gopnik, A. & Meltzoff, A. & Kuhl, P. (2001). *How Babies Think: The Science of Childhood*. London: Phoenix, Orion Publishing Group.

Guldberg, H. (2009). *Reclaiming Childhood. Freedom and play in an age of fear*. London: Routledge.

Harley, T. (2001). *The Psychology of Language. From data to theory*. 2nd Edition. Hove: Psychology Press Ltd.

Hunt, J. (2001). *The natural child*. Gabriola Island: New Society Publishers.

Kellmer-Pringle, M. (1986). *The Needs of Children. 3rd Edition*. London: Century Hutchinson.

Kitzinger, S. (2002). *Breastfeeding Your Way*. London: Dorling Kindersley.

Kitzinger, S. (2011). *Rediscovering Birth*. London: Little Brown.

Kitzinger, S. (2011). *The New Pregnancy and Childbirth: Choices & Challenges*. London: Dorling Kindersley.

Kline, N. (1998). *Time to Think: Listening to Ignite the Human Mind*. London: Cassell Illustrated.

Lucas, B. (2006). Happy Families; How to make one, how to keep one. BBC Active, Essex.

Macintyre, C. (2012). *Understanding Babies and Young Children from conception to three—a guide for students, practitioners and parents*. Oxford and New York: Routledge.

Mindgym. (2009). *Relationships*. London: Sphere.

Murkoff, H. & Eisenberg, A. & Hathaway, S. (2005). *What to expect the first year*. London: Simon & Schuster.

Parsloe, E. (1995). *Coaching to handle customers' problems*. Littleport: Fenman Ltd.

Passmore, J. & Pearson, D. (2011). *Seasons of Change: A coaching workbook for transition, redundancy and career change*. London: Chartered Management Institute.

Phelan, T. (2003). *1-2-3 Magic: Effective discipline for children 2–12*. United States: Child Management Inc.

Santrock, J. (2010). *Child development: An introduction*. New York: McGraw-Hill.

Satir, V. (2008). *Peoplemaking*. London: Souvenir Press Ltd.

Stone, E. (2002). *A Boy I Once Knew: What a Teacher Learned From Her Student*. Chapel Hill: Algonquin Books.

Sundin, J. (2008). *Birth Skills*. London: Vermilion.

Thomas, L. (2005). *The 7 Day Parent Coach*. London: Vermilion.

Waddilove, R. (2006). *The Baby Book; How to enjoy year one*. Oxford: Lion Hudson.

Waddilove, R. (2008). *The Toddler Book, How to enjoy your growing child*. Oxford: Lion Hudson.

West, Z. (2006). *Babycare Before Birth*. London: Dorling Kindersley.

Whitmore, J. (2009). *Coaching for Performance*. 4th Edition. London: Nicholas Brealey Publishing.

Wilson, A. (2005). *Listen to your children … and they will listen to you*. Rochester: Develop Your Child.

Witcraft, F. E. (1950). *Within My Power—The Power of One Man*. Irving: Scouting Magazine.

USEFUL CONTACTS AND WEBSITES

Action for Sick Children—healthcare charity formed to ensure that sick children always receive the highest standard of care possible.
Tel: 0800 0744 519
www.actionforsickchildren.org

Association for Spina Bifida and Hydrocephalus (ASBAH)—European organisation dedicated to supporting individuals and families facing challenges arising from spina bifida and hydrocephalus.
Tel: 01733 555988
www.asbah.org

BLISS—provides support and care to premature and sick babies.
Tel: 0500 618 140
www.bliss.org.uk

Cry-sis helpline—offers support for families with excessively crying, sleepless, and demanding babies.
Tel: 08451 228 669
www.cry-sis.org.uk

Daycare Trust—national childcare charity, campaigning for quality, accessible, affordable childcare for all and raising the voices of children, parents and carers.
Tel: 0845 872 6251
www.daycaretrust.org.uk

Direct Gov—public services website, including information on entitlements, childcare, schools, leisure, and legal rights.
www.direct.gov.uk/parents

Down's Syndrome Association—help for people with down's syndrome.
Tel: 0845 230 0372
www.downs-syndrome.org.uk

Family Lives—parenting advice and support charity.
Tel: 0808 800 2222
www.familylives.org.uk

Foundation for the Study of Infant Deaths—leading baby charity aimed at preventing unexpected deaths in infancy.
Tel: 0808 802 6868
www.fsid.org.uk

Gingerbread—provide expert advice and practical support, and campaign for single parents.
Tel: 0808 802 0925
www.gingerbread.org.uk

Inland Revenue—HM Revenue and Customs page providing information on tax credits and child benefits.
www.hmrc.gov.uk

La Leche League GB—mother-to-mother support for breastfeeding.
Tel: 0845 120 2918
www.laleche.org.uk

Multiple Births Foundation—healthcare professionals dedicated to supporting multiple birth families and educating and advising professionals about their special needs.
Tel: 020 3313 3519
www.multiplebirths.org.uk

Mumsnet—product reviews, parenting tips. and advice for parents.
www.mumsnet.com

National Childbirth Trust—the UK's largest parenting charity.
Tel: 0300 330 0770
www.nct.org.uk

National Childminding Association—helping families in England and Wales have access to high quality home-based childcare, play, learning, and family support.
Tel: 0845 880 0044
www.ncma.org.uk

Netmums—Parenting advice and information in your local area.
www.netmums.com

One Space—the parenting site for single parents providing information and support.
www.onespace.org.uk

Relate—Relate offers advice, relationship counselling, sex therapy, workshops, mediation, consultations, and support face-to-face, by phone and through their website.
Tel: 0300 100 1234
www.relate.org.uk

The Association for Post Natal Illness (APNI)—provides support to mothers suffering from post natal illness.
Tel: 0207 386 0868
www.apni.org

The Miscarriage Association—acknowledges the distress associated with pregnancy loss and strives to make a positive difference to those it affects.
Tel: 01924 200 799
www.miscarriageassociation.org.uk

Twins & Multiple Births Association (TAMBA)—providing support for families with twins, triplets, and more.
Tel: 01483 304442
www.tamba.org.uk

Working Families—helping working parents and carers achieve work/life balance.
Tel: 0800 013 0313
www.workingfamilies.org.uk

INDEX

For Product Safety Concerns and Information please contact our EU
representative GPSR@taylorandfrancis.com
Taylor & Francis Verlag GmbH, Kaufingerstraße 24, 80331 München, Germany

www.ingramcontent.com/pod-product-compliance
Lightning Source LLC
LaVergne TN
LVHW080655011026
849160LV00014B/1432
9781780491233